Wilderness Survival for Kids

A Comprehensive Guide to Finding Water, Foraging, Shelter Building, and More Essential Skills for Surviving in the Wild

Table of Contents

Introduction Letter to Parents

Thank you for choosing this exciting educational resource to add to your children's outdoor education and learning. This engaging book will empower your child with essential wilderness survival skills, all while keeping safety the top priority.

This comprehensive guidebook equips your child with the knowledge and skills needed when journeying in the great outdoors. Covering a range of topics, from preparing for wilderness adventures to handling emergencies and staying safe from wild animals, it serves as an educational tool, fostering a deeper connection to nature while teaching practical survival skills. Through easy-to-follow instructions, children learn valuable teamwork, problem-solving, and self-reliance lessons.

The safety of every child is the central concern. Your child is encouraged to practice these skills responsibly under adult supervision, ensuring a secure and controlled learning environment. While the book encourages outdoor exploration, it emphasizes the importance of staying safe and prepared for unexpected situations.

The book dives deep into various survival skills, including, but not limited to, finding water and wild edibles, starting fires, building shelters, staying safe around wild animals, creating useful tools, handling first aid and emergencies, learning navigation, and exploring additional survival hacks. These skills provide practical knowledge while instilling respect for the natural world and responsibility toward the environment.

Thank you for taking the time to nurture your child's outdoor education. Your child's safety and education are the top priorities. Enjoy this journey of exploration and learning, as there's nothing greater than discovering the wonders of the planet and one's own capabilities!

Introduction Letter to Children

It's great that you have chosen this book to guide you on this wild and wonderful journey. Here, you will learn about staying safe and surviving in the wilderness. You're about to become a true wilderness expert, and this book is your secret roadmap to all the incredible knowledge you need to enjoy the great outdoors safely. You will have so much fun learning some seriously cool stuff.

The first section of this awesome book prepares you for epic wilderness adventures. It's all about being ready for anything and making sure you have the right tools and knowledge to have a blast while staying safe. Then, you'll learn to find clean water and even delicious wild edibles.

That's not all, as the next section teaches you how to start a fire. You'll explore how to build your very own shelter. Whether it's a cozy den or a cool treehouse, you'll know how to create a safe space in the wild.

Guess what? In this book, you'll also learn how to stay safe around amazing wild animals. You'll know how to respect their space and enjoy nature without any worries. You'll be prepared to take action when it comes to first aid and emergencies. You can help in tricky situations and keep everyone safe with the knowledge you'll gain. This book is your guide to let you master navigation, so you'll always find your way back to camp or safety.

Every skill in this book comes with some awesome safety tips. You should follow these rules like they're your treasure map to adventure.

So, as you journey through the pages, remember that you're going to be safe, responsible, and - most of all - you will have a ton of fun. What are you waiting for? Get ready to explore, learn, and discover all the amazing things the great outdoors has to offer.

Section 1: Preparing for the Wilderness

If this is your first time experiencing the wilderness, you are right to be excited. This trip will be nothing short of an adventure. You'll get to be in the wild, running around freely, climbing trees, surrounded by animals and greenery, and doing all sorts of thrilling activities that nature offers. To get the most out of your natural escapade, you need to put some thought into the trip's preparations. Safety always comes first, and there is no safer way than being prepared for any surprises and armed with the knowledge of how to act in the face of danger or in an emergency.

It's a good idea to prepare an agenda. Do some research on the place you're going to, what it offers, and how to get there. You'd be surprised how many people reach their destinations only to find out there is an activity they wanted to do but haven't packed the gear needed for it because they didn't know it existed.

Part of preparation is asking others about their previous experiences, like a parent or a friend. Often, people don't learn important details about a situation until they've lived through it, which is a good chance for others to have the experience without the unpleasantness of going through it.

Destination Planning

First things first, where are you going?

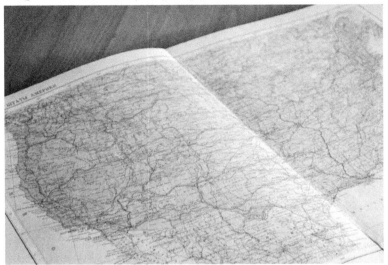

First, you need to decide on a destination.

Consider a few things while picking the national park you're heading to. How far is it? Will you need to commute, or will someone drive you? What's the weather going to be like? Is it safe to go without a parent or guardian? What sort of wildlife is there, and what precautions should you take to protect yourself against predators? There are many more questions that you need answers to before embarking on your quest.

Location

After you've picked out the destination, you'll need to research the area as much as you can. Most national parks have websites with information such as hiking trails and camping information. Check whether or not the area you're going to requires a permit to enter and, if so, how to get it.

Pick a place based on how long you're staying and how far you're willing to hike. If you'll be staying for a weekend, it's best to pick a site close to home so you don't spend half the trip on the road.

Take into consideration what you want to see, such as lakes, mountains, waterfalls, etc. You should also base your destination choice on the activities you want to do during your stay.

Check online for the maps of the trails and pick the one you want to tackle. Mark the campsites and water sources on the map in case you run low on supplies. Make sure you have GPS and a compass active on your phone, along with the physical map and compass. Save the locations on your phone for further reference while walking the trail.

If you're not going with a parent or a group, make sure that there is someone at home who knows where you'll be and how long you'll be gone. Set up check-in timings with them so they know you're okay.

Weather and Timing

Based on the time of year, you should be able to note the weather in the area unless it's in a different region. In that case, you'll need to check the forecast and the historic weather fluctuations.

Remember, in shaded areas, the temperatures drop quite low at night, so you need to pack your clothes accordingly.

Look for sun exposure, hours of daylight, and footwear information before you head out.

You'll need special boots and gear to move freely if there is snow. You'll also need to check if the trail is open because some trails close down during the snow season as a safety measure.

If you're going up a mountain, the temperature goes down the higher you go, and so does the oxygen level.

Summer trips are known for having the best weather, but this is also the most crowded time of year.

If you're a novice in camping, it is advised not to spend too much time on your first trip. 2 or 3 days is a good start to get the lay of the land and see how you like it, along with what works and what doesn't work for you.

The Company You Keep

Hiking is the perfect opportunity for bonding and getting to know others properly. People usually reveal their strengths and weaknesses when faced with adversity. They also come together and rely on one another when there is a challenge and no one else is around.

If you can't find someone to join you, you can post in the local trail discussion groups that you're looking for someone to hike with. Just make sure you inform your parents and give them the details of the person coming with you if they're not joining you.

Having company with you is not just for fun and games; it is preferred for safety reasons. If something unexpected is to happen, an injury, you get lost, or you lose some of your supplies, it's good to have someone along with backup to save the day.

When traveling with family, friends, or a group, the pace by which you move will be adjusted to accommodate the slowest person in the group. No one gets left behind.

Having someone along can also help reduce the weight you're carrying by sharing a tent, a kettle, and food.

Permit and Transportation

The more famous and popular the trail, the more likely you'll need to book a permit in advance. Some permits are immediate, but others may require months to secure a date. The popular spots employ *lottery-based permits*, meaning you must enroll months before your planned trip and wait to see if you're chosen.

Depending on the location, if you can't get a permit, there is sometimes an option to get a walk-up permit right before you hit the trail.

Not all trails allow backcountry camping (spread-out camping), which could mean you'll need to book separate campgrounds for the duration of your trip.

All the information you'll need on the permits should be found online, especially if it's a national or state forest.

As for the way you're going, that will depend on the distance. If it's a long drive or requires a flight, you're probably traveling with a camping group or your parents.

If you're somewhere nearby and safe enough to head out alone, you'll need someone to drop you off or take the shuttle.

Itinerary, Budget, and Rules

If you're going on a long trip, you need to plan for it.
https://unsplash.com/photos/six-white-sticky-notes--
1_RZL8BGBM?utm_content=creditShareLink&utm_medium=referral&utm_source=unsplash

Planning day-to-day activities is usually associated with longer trips. You don't usually need a detailed plan if the trip is only one or two days.

Your plan should include how far you'll walk every day, where you are camping, and what activities you'll do each day.

Long trips should include a rest day or an extra day if you don't have enough time to fit everything in.

Examine your supplies and food and see how much it'll cost to refill and buy anything you need. Also, consider that there may be transportation and permit costs.

When researching the park, pay attention to the rules and regulations posted. These rules keep you safe and give you the best experience possible during your stay. Look out for areas you need to stay clear of due to wild animals, a dangerous terrain that's been warned against, or a river known to have a strong current.

Be mindful of your surroundings, and always remember that you need to leave the area in the same, if not a better, condition than when you arrived. This means no littering, no cutting greenery, or damaging anything in the campsite, including the warning and direction signs.

Animals and Insects

In most areas, you don't need to worry about encountering any dangerous predators. The most likely appearances you'll encounter on your trip are raccoons, mice, and any form of rodents. However, you must pay attention to the warning signs at the park entrance or the start of the terrain.

In some areas, you may come across cougars, bears, or venomous snakes; in that case, the safest bet is to avoid that plot altogether.

If that is not an option, you must educate yourself on the safety measures to avoid injury or a life-threatening chase.

For example, if you're camping in a bear habitat, learn what to do if you come face to face with one and what type of bears are present. Also, learn how to store your food to keep it away from the bear, like using bear canisters.

You can count on meeting a few insects, so pack insect-repellent clothing and environment-friendly sprays to keep yourself bite-free.

You can also use a sleeping net as a hammock and mosquito nets during meal times to preserve your sanity.

Another way known among backpackers to keep mosquitos away is to wear rain gear.

Packing Your Outdoor Adventure Kit

If you're new to this, it's easy to be a little overwhelmed by the packing process. You don't want to over-pack to prevent walking around with an unnecessarily heavy load, and you don't want to play it so cool that you forget necessary items.

Each trip is different in terms of length, level of difficulty, location, and activities. However, there are some essential items you'll need to have on you for a successful trip:

Necessities

A compass is a necessary item when going to the wilderness.
https://unsplash.com/photos/round-white-compass-iDzKdNI7Qgc?utm_content=creditShareLink&utm_medium=referral&utm_source=unsplash

- Compass and a map (in case your phone dies and you need to figure out your way back or your next stopping point)
- Pocket flashlight for nighttime
- Multi-tool or a Swiss army knife
- Emergency blanket
- Tent
- Water flask and water filters for when you get to the water source
- Tools to start a fire, like a magnifying glass, lighter, matches, and lighter fluid
- A small bag to hold small items in your supplies
- First aid kit
- Sleeping bag
- Environment-friendly toiletries
- Trowel
- Repair tape
- If possible, a satellite phone, in case you're in an area with no bars

Clothing

- Hiking boots
- Hoodie or fleece
- Jacket
- Long underwear
- Waterproof attire
- Pairs of socks covering the period of the trip
- Hiking pants, shorts, and shirt
- Headwear for cold and hot weather
- Sandals for moving around the camp
- Sunglasses and sunscreen

Food

It's important to have a kettle in the wilderness.

Photo by laura adai on Unsplash https://unsplash.com/photos/stainless-steel-kettle-on-brown-wooden-table-lJHhM4D0wCU

- Lightweight stove and fuel
- Pots and utensils
- Sponge and soap (not to eat, to clean the pots with!)
- Spork, cup, and a bowl for each person
- Water, at least 32 ounces, should be on you at all times, along with the kit to purify water.
- Kettle
- Obviously, *food!*

Keep with you between 1.5 to 2.5 pounds of dry food per person. The effort you exert, and considering the speed you're moving, the elevation, and the distance, will drastically affect the amount you need to eat. Some people recommend that if you're new to backpacking, it won't hurt to over-pack food until you can ascertain your consumption and also in case of an emergency.

- Protein and energy bars, dried fruit, granola, and jerky.

Miscellaneous

- Equipment specific to the activities you want to partake in. A bicycle, if there is biking terrain. Kayak, if you're into rowing down river streams. Walking poles for hiking. If you're going during the snow season, then ski equipment and swim trunks, or if you're going swimming in a lake or river.
- Electronics, phones, cameras, headphones, iPod, and battery-based chargers.
- Have some fun items on you, like astrology books, games, stories, a journal or your sketchbook, and a coloring kit.

Emergency Tools and First Aid

Prepare yourself for the outdoors with first aid and emergency training. Being aware of when you are in a tight situation and how to act accordingly and appropriately can be the difference between ending up with a band-aid and being airlifted to a hospital.

Signaling

There are a lot of signals used in survival training. All rescue personnel are aware of the meanings and the different nature of each one, making this tool one of the most effective in alerting the authorities that you need help.

These signals include fire, flashing lights, mirrors, flags, colored markers, and whistles.

As most search and rescue uses helicopters, aircraft, and maybe drones, it's a good idea to form your signals in an open area so they're easily discovered.

For instance, if you form three fires in a triangle, this can be interpreted as a distress signal, especially if a drone or a helicopter is flying by. Make sure your fires are carefully banked to prevent setting the surrounding shrubbery on fire.

You can also use mirrors to alert people on planes or from a long distance from your location. They are hard to miss when angled properly with the sun or using a flashlight.

You can use a strobe light at night to alert those nearby in the camping area. You can also generate smoke during the day from fire using organic materials.

Another way to send a signal is to use rocks, logs, and bright-colored clothing by laying them down on the ground and spelling out the word S.O.S. These signals are clear to any airborne craft.

First Aid

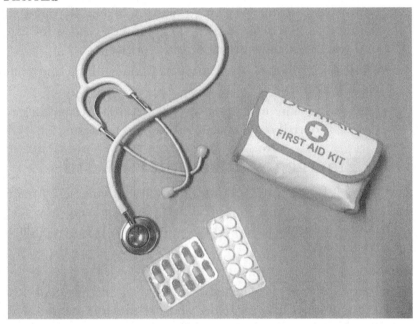

Having a first aid kit and being able to use it are two different things.
https://unsplash.com/photos/a-bag-of-pills-a-stethoscope-and-a-first-aid-kit-ZyxNWi3JCto?utm_content=creditShareLink&utm_medium=referral&utm_source=unsplash

First aid doesn't just include the bandages and antiseptic you have on you. A primary component of survival is your attitude. You need to stay calm and collected. Do not let your panic grab the steering wheel. Use STOP, which stands for Sit, Think, Observe, and Plan.

Implement logic, assess your situation, and determine what you need to safely escape it.

It is important to detail the medical equipment you'll need. If you have a specific condition, like diabetes or IBS, make sure you have the medication for that. If you have allergies or suspect you may be allergic to anything in the wilderness, have antihistamines with you just in case. These should be packed safely in waterproof containers, which are kept safely on you at all times.

Don't forget to include the basics, like dressings for small cuts and bruises. If there are any items in the kit you've never used before, you need to go over how to safely administer these items.

You can protect yourself against hypothermia by using a space blanket at night. Make sure your gear is labeled, and you have a family picture on you with your address written on the back and a contact number so that if you're lost or lose your things, whoever finds them has a place to start looking from.

If there is something you don't understand or don't know how or when to use it, do not hesitate to ask an adult to show you and explain it to you.

Final Sweep

Once you're all packed, go over everything you have, from the things you packed to the documents you need to make sure you're not missing anything.

- Lift your bag to get a feel of its heaviness. There is a good chance you won't need that extra can of beans once you feel its weight on your back.
- Double-check the weather to avoid any unwanted surprises. While some people love going out in the rain or during storms and damp weather, this may not be the best idea for someone still finding their footing in the wilderness. If there is an unfavorable change in the forecast, consider canceling or postponing the trip until things get better.
- Share your plans with people you trust, like your parents, guardians, or close friends. If you have a satellite phone, provide them with the number. Also, leave your details in several places within your gear in case you need to be found.
- Make sure you have an evacuation route marked in case of an emergency or unforeseen weather.

Section 2: Water and Wild Edibles

Staying hydrated and well-nourished while exploring the outdoors is vital to enjoying the experience. You won't be having fun if you feel too weak to move or partake in activities. A big part of Boy Scouts' training is finding clean water and edible food on your own in the wild. Why, may you ask? Well, there are several scenarios where you may need this training.

These scenarios may involve under-packing your food, losing some of it, or being overly generous when sharing it with the forest critters. You could get lost, or a bear steals your food.

In both cases, you need to be armed with the knowledge of how to keep yourself alive by acquiring food and water from natural sources.

Remember, just because you're about to learn how to gather water and food from the wild doesn't mean you should forgo preparing and packing for your potential needs.

You should only resort to natural sources if you absolutely have to.

Water

Assume you lost your water flask, it broke, or you drank all the water you have and still have a long way to go. Keep calm, and don't panic. Survival depends on decisions made in the first few minutes of realizing an emergency. Making a decision out of fear will only make matters worse.

Don't worry about losing your water flask; make a way to tote it or keep up with it. Survival is all about making decisions in an emergency.

Start by monitoring your body's response to the environment. Is it cool where you are? Are you sweating profusely? Is your body losing water quickly, or can you last a while longer without a water source?

Now that you've settled down and assessed your situation, you can start the search for drinking water. The three primary types of water you'll be looking for are surface water, like rivers and lakes, groundwater from springs, and rainwater.

Pay Attention

Remember that water collected from lakes, rivers, or plant condensation must be filtered and purified. It is not safe to drink water straight from the source. However, if faced with a life-or-death situation, then you'll probably have no choice besides biting the bullet and taking that risk. Just be aware that any water you drink that hasn't been through a filtration process will most likely have bacteria. Also, be mindful that some techniques used in collecting water make it safer to drink than others.

Remember, it is always better to target running water whenever you can. The flow of the river or stream makes it hard for bacteria to manifest and spread. So, your number one choice should be small streams and underground reservoirs. Rivers come in next, but note that they may carry pollution from upstream. Always collect water as close to the upstream as possible where the current is fast. Lakes and ponds are an acceptable choice. However, they have a higher chance of bacterial presence because of the stagnant water.

Just because the water is clear doesn't mean it's safe to drink. Look for signs of life. If there aren't any around, not even algae, do not drink it. It won't be safe. Also, avoid water sources where rats are present.

Rivers and Streams

This is an excellent exercise to train your ninja senses. Stand perfectly still, close your eyes, and listen. Water sounds can sometimes be heard even if the source is pretty far away.

Now, open your eyes and try to locate any animal tracks. Although a damper on camping, a swarm of insects indicates nearby water. A bird's flight path also leads to bodies of water. So, keep your eyes peeled and your ears to the ground.

Take a look around you and notice the terrain you're on. Water runs downwards, so follow any valleys you see and look out for ravines or ditches. If you arrive at low ground, you're likely to find water.

Underground Water

Underground water signs can include dried river beds and wet dirt. Notice if there are any signs of green vegetation, like shrubs, which are common around water sources. Look for animals assembling in one area. This usually indicates water is below the surface.

Start digging until you feel the sand or dirt getting wet, then wait until the water seeps into the hole.

Be sure to purify the water you gather from the hole you dug.

Rain Water and Morning Dew

Rain is probably one of the safest and easiest methods of collecting water, and as long as you're not in a heavily industrialized area (where rain turns acidic), you're probably safe. You can use a tarp, tree leaves, or even your own clothing to gather the rain. The water gathered from this source is usually pure and needs minimal purification.

You can also find some droplets trapped between the leaves and stems of plants following the rain.

You may think that morning dew is a very small amount of water that won't make that much of a difference. However, these small droplets can easily add up to substantial amounts of drinking water. This is especially true in grassy areas.

Be sure to start collecting early in the morning before the sun rises and the water evaporates. You can tie a cloth around your ankles or wrists and walk around in a tall grassy area. The dew will be caught in the cloth, and then you can wring out the water into your container.

Another source similar to the morning dew is the *Sphagnum* moss. These plants grow close to the ground and are often located in damp areas, under the shade of trees away from the light. The moss collects water quite well, and you can retrieve it by pulling apart a clump and squeezing it to release the liquid.

Snow and Ice

Snow and ice are abundantly available in areas of high altitude and colder weather. As straightforward as this sounds, there are a few things to be cautious about.

Don't ever drink ice or snow in huge quantities all at once. This has the potential to lower your body temperature drastically and suddenly and can cause hypothermia.

Melt the ice first. Place it in a pan; add more when the first batch has melted.

Purifying the Water

- Boiling - A common method is using a cloth to filter out any large bits of sediment and then boiling the water. Bacteria cannot withstand high temperatures, so 10 minutes over the fire should do it.

However, you need a container of some sort to start a fire. If you can't find a traditional container, use a plastic bottle, tin can, aluminum can, glass jar, or a large shell. Now, you might worry that the plastic bottle will melt, but if you fill it to the brim and tightly close it, the lack of air should stop the damage. You can also suspend it in the air above the fire.

If you can't start a fire, place the water in the sun in a clear flask to kill the bacteria.

- **Filtration Pumps:** These pumps are filters you can find in any camping store. The water passes over a ceramic or charcoal filter that treats any impurities in it, sometimes using chemicals as well. The end result is pure, drinkable water when you're stuck outdoors.

- **Purification Tablets and Drops:** This is a simple and cheap way to clean water collected from the wild. All you have to do is add a couple of tablets or drops to your water container, wait for 20 minutes, and voila! You have drinking water. The tablets usually contain iodine, chlorine, potassium, and permanganate. You can also add powdered mixes to mask the taste.

  Always consult a doctor before using these, as they may cause medical issues if you are sensitive to any of the components or if you have a specific medical condition. Also, the chlorine used to purify the water is different from the tablets used for the pool, so don't use those.

- **Use Plants:** Some plants in the wild are purifying agents. However, you must familiarize yourself with them because a simple mistake can have dire consequences. These plants include xylem, rice and coconuts, cilantro, fruit and banana peels, Oregon grape, and many others.

  Soak these plants in your water and seal them together. The plants will naturally work on clearing and purifying your water.

- **Sedimentation:** This is a no-brainer. If you place your water in a container and leave it stagnant, the impurities are bound to sink to the bottom. All you need to do is scoop the water up without disturbing it so it doesn't get mixed together again.

Water Containers

When choosing the containers to store your water in, you'll find there are quite a few options. If you're carrying a lot of luggage and don't want to add to the weight, a handy and cheap option is plastic water bottles, though they don't offer much when it comes to durability.

If you want a sturdier option, go for water jugs. They're a bit heavier but more environmentally friendly than plastic bottles. Remember not to leave plastic bottles in a natural environment.

You can always use specialized containers. These are tailored to the camping crowd, easy to carry, and durable, but they cost a little bit extra. However, if you consider how long they last, you'll find that they are a good investment.

Wild Edibles

One of the first golden rules of gathering food from Mother Nature is to only eat what you know is safe. If you can't identify it, don't eat it.

The process of locating sustenance from the wild is called foraging. Many campers and wildlife enthusiasts rely on this process for food and sometimes medicine, especially if they stay outdoors for long periods.

Specialists implement edibility tests to be sure that what they're eating is not toxic or poisonous.

Consider having a field guide of the area with details of the wild edibles and the poisonous and toxic plants.

So, how does one forage?

Edible Options

Humans can go a long time without eating, so don't risk it unless you're sure of what you're putting in your body. However, there are some go-to safe options to boost your energy levels if need be.

    • **Berries**

Mulberries are edible 99% of the time.

Berries are a really good source of carbs, vitamins, and fiber. Look for the ones packed together tightly, like raspberries and mulberries (also known as aggregate berries). Those are edible 99% of the time. It is recommended to do an edibility test regardless of how certain you are about what you're eating.

Blue, black, and purple berries are around 90% edible. Orange and red berries are 50% edible, and green, white, and yellow berries are 10% edible, so stay away from that last one and do not take the risk, not even with an edibility test.

• **Greens**

There are obvious options, like fruit and vegetables. However, if you can't find those, your next best bet is weed. Many weed-like plants, like dandelion, clover, chicory, cattail, lamb's quarters, amaranth, nettles, purslane, sorrel, and mustard, are edible.

A highly recommended option is onions. Just make sure it looks and smells like an onion. If it doesn't, put it down. Also, anything that smells like almonds but doesn't look like almonds is a red flag.

• **Insects**

Believe it or not, insects contain seven times the amount of protein found in ground beef!

If you are forced down that road, the safe options to try are earthworms, ants (boil those first in case they're fire ants), crickets, grasshoppers (remove legs and wings), and mealworms.

• **Birds and Snakes**

Pigeons are safe to eat.
https://www.pexels.com/photo/flock-of-flying-pigeons-2407721/

If you're up for it and know how to catch birds, go for it. Pigeons, crows, or seagulls are all safe to eat.

With snakes, though, it's a bit tricky. Stay away from any venomous ones. If you can't 100% tell if it is poisonous, do not attempt to catch it.

• **Marine Life**

Small fish in lakes or rivers, such as isopods, freshwater crustaceans, and oysters, are edible.

Poisonous Plants

Examples of poisonous plants are poison hemlock, foxglove, water hemlock, poison oak, or poison ivy. When you're out in the wild, you must be able to identify the marks of a dangerous plant. Some of these marks are easy to spot without the help of a field guide.

• **Waxy Leaves:** The wax present on the leaves of some plants can be a simple indicator that it has a protective layer that retains water. However, it can also indicate that this plant is toxic. Anything with leaves resembling parsley, dill, or parsnip is probably poisonous.

- **Milky Sap:** This is a substance that oozes out of the plant when the stem breaks. It can cause skin irritation and allergic reactions.

- **Mushrooms:** You need to be able to identify mushrooms with absolute certainty. Morel, oyster, and chanterelle mushrooms are safe and edible. If you can't name it, don't pick it. Don't be tempted by the fungi growing on trees or on the ground.

- **Umbrella-Shaped Flower Clusters:** Most of these umbrella-shaped flowers are toxic and should be avoided at all costs.

- **Fine Hairs and Spines:** Plants with these characteristics usually have a defense mechanism against predators. In this case, the predator is you. A lot of these hairs can sting and burn once you touch them.

- **Trust the Taste:** If you taste the plant and are *struck with a bitter or soapy taste*, spit it out immediately. Poisonous plants always taste bad.

- **Bright Colors:** Insects, plants, marine life, whatever it is, stay away from anything with bright colors.

Edibility Test

There is a way to test plants when you're not 100% sure whether or not they are edible (like orange berries).

- **Rule out the Poisonous Traits:** Go through the previously mentioned poison indicators before examining them further.

- **Skin Test:** Rub a piece of the plant on your forearm or outer lip. Wait for about 15 minutes to see if there is a reaction.

- **Taste Test:** If there is no skin reaction, taste the same bit you tested on your skin. Wait for another 5 minutes.

- **Take a Bigger Taste Test:** If there is no reaction and you don't taste any bitterness, soapy flavor, or almond flavor or feel any numbness, take a bigger bite, the size of a teaspoon, and then wait 8 hours.

- **Eat a Bit More:** If you're still not suffering from any digestive issues, eat another teaspoon and wait another 8 hours. If nothing happens, you can consider that part of the plant edible in the state in which you performed the taste test (raw, cooked, dried).

- **Be Careful:** Be mindful, and use your common sense. If you're unsure what you're eating, don't take an unnecessary risk. The human body can survive 30 days without food and three without water.

Many of the edible options have poisonous twins. Sometimes, the fruit is edible, but the stems and leaves aren't. Just because one part is safe doesn't mean all of it is. Only eat the bit you tested and are sure it is edible.

Section 3: Starting a Fire

Not the arson kind! Burning things to a crisp is the only drawback of fire. If you take care, it doesn't destroy or spread and will prove to be one of your most useful allies in the wilderness. Fire can cook your food, decontaminate your water, signal for help, keep wild animals at bay, and provide warmth and light. Armed with the knowledge of starting a fire, your chances of survival in the wilderness rise significantly. Furthermore, you don't need to pack anything extra to start a fire in the woods. All the required tools will be available in nature, but it always helps to keep a match or a lighter handy.

Starting a fire can help you cook and decontaminate water.

Key Elements

As you may know, fire is the result of the combustion process. It is a reaction between three key elements: fuel, oxygen, and heat. It is called the "fire triangle".

- **Fuel**

  Fuel can be anything that combusts upon the addition of heat. Materials like paper, wood, clothes, certain liquids and gasses, rubber, etc. can be used as fuel. Materials that don't burn are not considered fuel. For instance, an iron rod will melt after adding a certain amount of heat but not combust.

- **Oxygen**

  Oxygen is a naturally occurring element that is available all around us. Fuel burns due to a reaction with oxygen. Without the presence of oxygen in the atmosphere, you cannot light a fire, even if you have the other two parts of the triangle. Therefore, you cannot start a fire on the moon because there is no oxygen, but you definitely can in the Earth's wilderness.

- **Heat**

  Just as oxygen helps you survive, heat helps fire thrive. You simply cannot start a fire without the presence of heat. You cannot just use the heat from the atmosphere, however. For practical purposes, you will need an ignition source that will produce a spark of heat at a much higher temperature, like a match.

Fire Safety Precautions

Imagine that you successfully lit a fire in a forest. You gave it enough fuel to last for hours and left it unattended as you snuggled in your blanket for a good night's sleep. Over time, the dry leaves near the burning fuel catch fire, quickly spreading all around. The crackling of combustion and the excess heat wake you up. Due to the lack of a water source nearby, you frantically think about what to do next. At a complete loss, you run from the place and out of the woods. Eventually, the nearby trees will catch fire, too, and in a matter of hours, the entire forest will be burning with fierce intensity.

Don't let this eventuality frighten you from starting a fire in the wilderness. There are several ways to avoid the drawbacks of fires. Take these few good precautions.

- **Dig a Fire Pit**

  Most campsites already have fire pits in specific places. If there isn't one, feel free to pick up a shovel and dig, as long as campfires are allowed. Choose an open area with no trees around or above. Are you bang in the middle of the forest? Pick a spot where the nearest tree branches are far above the ground. Sweep a few feet of the area clear. Make sure there aren't any leaves or combustible materials around. Then, start digging the pit until it is roughly eight inches deep.

- **Water Source**

  It is recommended to start a fire near a water source, like a river or a lake, so you can readily douse the flames if something other than the pit's contents catches fire. If you are far from a water source, keep a bucket full of water or a fire blanket on hand.

- **Place Rocks around the Fire**

  Despite the above two precautions, there is still a chance for the fire to spread. To minimize that chance, place rocks around the pit in a circle, enclosing any gaps with smaller stones.

Identifying and Collecting Suitable Firewood/Fuel

You can purchase firewood from a coal shop or a furniture store, but carrying it all the way to the spot isn't exactly feasible. Many campsites are equipped with firewood and other fuel sources. Do you want an authentic wilderness experience instead? Identify the right type of fuel in the vicinity and collect it yourself. Whatever you collect, make sure it's dry. Wet stuff doesn't catch fire. It's stubborn that way.

- Look for fallen twigs or branches, especially in a place where there are a lot of trees.
- Cut down low-hanging tree branches.
- Peel off tree barks that are already jutting out.

- In stony, mountainous regions, you may find firewood underneath rocks.

- Branches from a dead tree are devoid of moisture, perfect for kindling a fire. Its rotting part provides a tinder, and you can use the trunk of a fallen tree as fuel logs.

- Dry leaves and pine needles are perfect sources of tinder.

- You may need to climb a tree to find dry firewood in wet conditions. The sun's rays evaporate moisture quickly from the topmost branches.

Arranging the Firewood

You can simply dump the fuel into the fire pit and light it up. However, it won't be efficient and may fizzle out after a few minutes. You don't want all the hours you spent collecting firewood to go to waste. There are several ways to arrange firewood for efficient combustion. Here are three of the most common arrangements.

- **Teepee Fire**

A teepee fire.

If you have been camping for a while, you may know what a teepee (also spelled as tipi) tent looks like. It's a conical shelter held together with wooden poles and covered with a cloth. Your teepee fire will be structurally similar, except made of logs, branches, twigs, and tinder.

1. Place the tinder at the center of the pit.
2. Cover it with small branches in the form of a teepee tent. Grab a few branches in one palm, hold the top, and arrange the bottom around the tinder in a cone.
3. Finally, place the fuel logs around the branches in a cone. Leave enough space between each log to maintain constant airflow.

• **Lean-to Fire**

As the name suggests, a lean-to fire leans onto something (in this case, a log or a tree trunk). It doesn't need a fire pit and can be kindled even in strong wind. The trunk provides excellent cover.

1. Position the log or the trunk perpendicular to the wind direction.
2. Place the tinder so that the log face protects it from the wind.
3. Arrange twigs and branches on top of it, with one end leaning on the log.
4. Add bigger logs to provide better cover.

• **Log Cabin Fire**

This is a more robust type of arrangement. It protects your fire from the wind and provides a base for you to place a kettle or a bowl for cooking. The contraption is square-shaped, with an opening at the base to light the tinder.

1. Place the tinder or kindling in a bunch on the floor.
2. Arrange two logs horizontally opposite each other. They must be of the same width.
3. Place two more logs on top at a right angle to each. Make sure the tinder within is visible from the top.
4. Similarly, place two more logs at a right angle to the second base. You may construct another story the same way.

Fire-Starting Methods

Once you have dug a fire pit, taken all the precautions, collected the right fuel (tinder, twigs, logs, etc.), and arranged them in your preferred style, it's time to start a fire. The easiest and safest way is to strike a match and drop it on the tinder/kindling at the base. Don't try to light the covering branches or logs. They will take a long time to catch fire, and you will end up wasting several matchsticks.

If you use a lighter instead, you must be very careful since you cannot just drop it on the tinder. Never lower the lighter from the top. When the tinder catches fire, it will burn your hand. Approach from the sides. In a teepee fire, you won't be able to access the tinder easily. You must remove the branches and logs from a small section to reach it with your lighter. With lean-to and log cabin fires, there is enough space on the sides to get your lighter near the tinder.

Did you forget to pack both matches and lighter? No sweat. Here are a few other innovative yet safe ways to start a fire.

- **Magnifying Glass**

  This is probably the most exciting way to start a fire. Remember the time you used a magnifying glass to focus the sun's rays and heat things up (bowl of water or a piece of paper) just for fun? That is exactly how you can light the tinder.

A magnifying glass can help you start a fire.

  Hold the magnifying glass so the sun's rays converge on the tinder. Make as small a point as possible. Within a few minutes, the tinder will begin to smoke, and a few more seconds later, a visible flame will burst into life. As you may have figured out, you can use this technique only during the day under sufficient sunlight, not in the dark of the night.

- **Batteries**

This is an old-fashioned way of starting a fire. You will need a battery with both terminals on one side (not easily available today, hence old-fashioned). You will also need to buy steel wool from a convenience store. Rub the battery terminals on the wool. Make sure you are holding a good thick stack. Otherwise, you may burn your hand. As you rub the terminals on the steel wool, you'll create a spark that will light up the wool. Drop it on the tinder and blow gently on it. After a few seconds, a blazing fire will start.

- **Flint and Steel**

Did you know that flint and steel were first used to start a fire as far back as the 11th century? All you need is a flint rock (usually found near a river), a char cloth (a piece of cloth made of charcoal), and a steel knife. This method will need adult supervision.

Place the char cloth on the flint and hold them together near the edge. Strike the cloth with the knife blade far away from your fingers. After a few good strikes, the cloth will catch fire. Drop it onto the tinder and blow.

Tending the Fire

After starting the fire, you cannot leave it as is. It will burn bright initially, but the intensity will reduce as time passes until it completely dies down. You need to tend the fire occasionally to keep it burning for a long time. Tending simply means that you should place more firewood on it. Add kindling materials like twigs and sticks.

Putting out the Fire

The most important step in starting a fire is being able to put it out. You don't want your camping spot to go up in flames. Admittedly, if you keep the fire untended and leave the spot, it may fizzle out after a while, but there is a high chance it will spread to the surrounding area. However, you can't just pour a bucket full of water on it and leave. You need to ensure that the fire is indeed extinguished. It's a three-step process:

1. Fill your water bucket to the brim and drain it on the burning tinder.

2. Scoop up a handful of soil from the ground and drop it on the doused area. A shovel is recommended for this purpose.

3. Hold your hands (palms facing down) over the pit.

Are you feeling the heat? Then the fire hasn't completely gone out. Stir the residue with a long stick to locate any burning embers. Then, repeat the three-step process again and again until you cannot feel the heat. At this point, ask an adult to touch the ashen, wet residue to be sure the fire has been extinguished. If it's hot, you will need to repeat the three-step process.

That's not all. Follow the "leave no trace" principle. Scatter the ashes in the surrounding area or sweep them off into a corner of the clearing. Remove the stones from around the pit and cover it with soil. Only then will you have successfully put out the fire.

Section 4: Shelter Building

From the basic necessities of wilderness survival, you have already taken care of two. You have packed the right clothes for the adventure and learned how to find food and water to cook on your fire. It's time to tackle the third and final necessity, building a shelter.

The primary use of a wilderness shelter is to protect yourself from the elements. You don't have to construct a log cabin or a fully-fledged house with a lock. You are out in the wilderness with a group of children or adults, so you don't have to worry about thieves. All you need is a roof on your head and makeshift walls on the sides to shield yourself from wind, rain, snow, and heat.

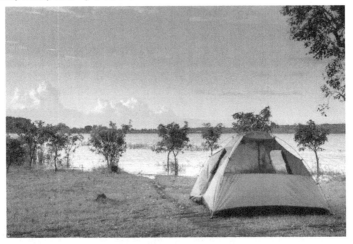

A tent will add to your heavy baggage.
https://www.pexels.com/photo/camping-dome-tent-near-a-body-of-water-2582818/

While you can carry a tent with you, it will only add to your already heavy baggage. Even collapsible tents are bulky and require a lot of space. Wouldn't creating your own shelter from materials readily available in the wilderness would be less cumbersome? Plus, it will be a whole lot of fun!

Shelter Essentials

You don't need a tent to build a proper tent-like shelter. All you need is a tarp and a rope. The rest of the essentials can be found in a natural environment. A rope is a necessary component of your wilderness kit. It has many uses, from shelter building to climbing up or down steep inclines. A tarp, on the other hand, is almost exclusively used for shelter building. Don't want to add it to your burden? Perfectly understandable. You can still make a shelter entirely out of things from the wild. You will need:

- A long, thick tree branch or a log
- Around 20 similar-length branches that are smaller than the main branch
- Lots and lots of dry leaves or pine needles as cover

Why Use a Tarp, Dry Leaves, or Pine Needles?

When building a shelter, you should ensure protection against all elements. The weather may be unpredictable in the wild. There may be scorching heat for one hour, followed by a dense cloud and a deluge of rain the next. If you plan to climb to the top of a mountain, you may even experience stormy winds and incessant snowfall.

A tarp acts as the perfect shelter against all elements. It won't let rain or snow get to you, it will protect you from the burning heat, and if it has been tied properly, it will remain stable in the wind.

A tarp shelters you from all elements.

Dry leaves are an ideal protection against extreme heat and cold. They keep the inside of your shelter cool as a cucumber in hot weather and warm as sunbeams on a chilly winter night. Rain won't be a problem if you have enough leaf layers stacked on top of each other. In a downpour, your shelter will remain as dry as if it hadn't rained at all!

Furthermore, you don't need to carry a camping bed or an air mattress with you. Multiple layers of dry leaves stacked within the shelter provide enough ground elevation and comfort. Pine needles have the same advantages as dry leaves.

Building Different Types of Shelters

Building a shelter out of naturally available materials is a lot like creating different types of fire arrangements, as you learned in the previous chapter. The easiest types of shelters to build are the lean-to and log cabin tents.

• Lean-to Shelter

Drawing of a lean-to shelter.
https://commons.wikimedia.org/wiki/File:Field-expedient_lean-to_and_fire_reflector.jpg

You may remember that a lean-to type of fire consists of several branches propped up against a big log. The method of constructing this type of shelter is similar, but you also need to prop the big log up against a tree for better elevation.

1. Find a strong log or tree trunk a little longer than your height.

2. Pick a tree with a strong branch near the ground.

3. Rest one end of the log against the branch and let the other end fall to the ground. It will look like the hypotenuse of a right-angled triangle.

4. Place one end of the similar-length branches on the log, one beside the other, and let the other end rest on the ground. Do this only on one side of the log and leave the other side open. It will make a sort of slanted cave.

5. Place a large bunch of leaves or pine needles on the ground inside the shelter. Make sure there are enough by checking that your body doesn't touch the ground when you lie on them.

6. Place more leaves or pine needles on the branches so that not a single ray of sunlight falls into the cave from that side.

Pro Tip: you can keep warm at night in your lean-to shelter by starting a fire a couple of feet ahead of the open side.

• Log Cabin Shelter

This is more of a bed than a shelter, but it is extremely effective. Do you remember the log cabin fire in the previous chapter? The method of constructing this shelter is similar. You will need a large pile of logs and branches, along with a big bunch of pine needles.

1. Pick a spot under the shade of a tree.
2. Place two logs parallel to each other at a distance of a little more than your height.
3. Add two long logs or branches on top of the base logs so they are perpendicular, and the distance between them is a little more than your breadth.
4. Add two more sets of logs to complete the structure.
5. Fill the base of this makeshift log cabin with pine needles. Make sure it's comfortable to lie on.
6. Once you're lying down, ask your friend or an adult to cover your body with more pine needles. Leave your face uncovered.

You will be fast asleep in this ultra-comfy shelter within minutes! You can also replace the pine needles with dry leaves if you want.

• Tarp Shelter

A tarp tent isn't the all-natural shelter you want during your wilderness adventure, but it is the fastest to build, and it has the capability of protecting you against all elements. You may know what a tarp shelter looks like. It's usually an inverted V suspended on a rope and affixed to the ground with more ropes. Where there are ropes, there are knots. You should learn two basic types of knots to be able to build a tarp shelter.

• **Taut Line Hitch:** It's mostly used to tie the tarp ends to hooks or trees. (pictures showing each step of the taut line hitch knot)

- **Running Bowline:** It's used to hang the ridgelines to trees.

Ideally, you can use a taut line hitch to tie up the entire tent, but learning a few more knots doesn't hurt! The long ropes on the tarp may become loose over time. Try tying a Prusik knot near the middle.

Follow these steps to build the perfect tarp shelter.

1. A tarp is generally available as a square. If it isn't, cut it into that shape.

2. A hole in each corner will be present as well. If there isn't, punch an inch-wide hole.

3. Find two trees a few feet apart (ideally, a little longer than the length of your tarp). You will build your shelter between them.

4. Connect the two trees with a rope at a height of a couple of inches more than half your tarp. You will be using a running bowline knot on the two ends.

5. Place the tarp over the rope so that it goes through the midpoints of the tarp's sides.

6. Tie a rope through each hole of the four corners with a taut line hitch knot. The other end of each rope should also be a taut line hitch.

7. Affix four small but strong twigs with miniature spikes into the ground at sufficient distances from the tarp's corners. Make sure the tarp will stretch after it's connected to the twigs. Ask an adult for help. If you can't find any twigs, you can use steel hooks.

8. Connect the open taut line hitches to the hooks, and your tarp shelter is ready!

Finding the Right Materials in Nature for Your Shelter

When looking for twigs, logs, branches, leaves, and pine needles, did you imagine yourself collecting them from live trees? That's a bad idea. It may snap while pulling down a low-hanging branch, and tiny, sharp wood pieces may pierce your skin. Chopping down trees for logs with an axe is highly unsafe for children. Furthermore, neither of these options is environmentally friendly. You should always respect nature, not harm it. So, how can you find the right materials to build your shelter?

The answer is simple. Look for dead trees or branches that have already fallen to the ground. In a forest, you may find quite a few of those. Is the bark of the trunk peeling off easily? Is its color white and unhealthy looking? Does it lack leaves on its branches? That's a dead tree for you.

Before carrying off the branches and logs, look for any sharp edges or spikes. Use a knife to prune the branch or ask an adult to do so. Dead branches and tree trunks are usually infested with pests and insects. Carry only those branches that have little to no infestation. It implies that the wood is strong enough to hold your shelter upright for a long time.

Dry leaves and fallen pine needles can be found in any wilderness region in the fall season. If it's not that time of the year yet, you can find a bunch in the arboretum section of the forest, a place where there is a nursery of plants. Alternatively, ask the forest officials where they store dry leaves after sweeping the forest floor.

If you find neither dry leaves nor pine needles, you can pluck dead grass from the vicinity of your camp. Only if you can't find anything else should you consider using live trees as the source of materials for your shelter. Make sure not to pluck anything from any rare or endangered species of plants and trees. Keep away from the poisonous plants. Avoid any plant or tree you cannot identify, or ask an adult for help.

Adapting Your Shelter for Different Weather Conditions

In the wilderness, the weather can change abruptly and dramatically. A light rain can transform into stormy winds. The leaves of your lean-to shelter probably won't stay put. Is the wind continuously lashing at your tarp from a fixed direction? Your tent may be leaning more to one side. Here are a couple of solutions to adapt to the changing weather conditions.

- **Build a Hut**

    A lean-to shelter is covered only on one side. The other side is wide open. What if the wind and rain change direction suddenly and come at you from the open side? Additionally, what if you want more privacy in your shelter? You don't have to build a specialized hut for this purpose. Just cover the other side, too!

Collect more branches and leaves and let them lean on the open side. Make sure there is enough space from the direction of the main tree for you to crawl in. If not, remove a few branches and leaves from both sides on that end.

There is a small drawback to transforming your lean-to shelter into a hut. You cannot light a fire. You don't want to risk lighting it near the open end either because of the tree. You will have to decide what matters the most to you, your privacy or the comforting heat of a fire.

• **Make a Lean-to Tarp**

Just like you made a hut from a lean-to shelter, you can convert your tarp hut into a lean-to tarp. If the wind is especially fierce from one side, you can cover that side almost entirely with this transformation.

1. Unhook the two corners of one side of your tarp shelter (the one opposite the wind direction).

2. Tie the two corners to the main rope at either end. You can also tie them to the two trees with running bowline knots.

3. Pull out the hooks from the remaining two corners and pull them further back until the tarp is fully stretched.

4. Push the hooks back into the ground at those points.

Voila! Your lean-to tarp shelter is ready. It will be much more spacious than the tarp hut and better protect you from the one-sided wind or rain.

Section 5: Staying Safe from Wild Animals

Reading this chapter, you will learn how animals play a role in the world around you. You'll understand the importance of treating them with respect and giving them their space, and know how you can do it. This chapter also provides tips for how to hike safely and respect other people and wildlife while you're on the trail. Finally, you will know how to identify common types of wildlife and learn safety precautions.

Why Understanding and Respecting Wildlife Is Important

How do you behave when you're invited to someone's house? You probably avoid making a mess and being loud, right? You listen to and follow the house's rules, sit on chairs rather than countertops, and admire their decor and paintings without taking anything home. After dinner, you help with the dishes and clean up the toys before you leave.

Protect the ecosystem by respecting its wildlife.

Visiting the wilderness is a lot like visiting someone's house. You become a guest in the homes of wildlife and must act as you would at someone else's house and how you expect others to act when they're at your place. In the wild, you should avoid making a mess and being so loud that you disturb animals and put yourself at risk. You should also sit on benches or other durable objects and clean up when you leave. You admire the animals and their habitat without taking anything home, even if it's just a shell or a log. If you do that, you may accidentally be taking away someone's home.

Maintaining the Ecosystem

Think of the ecosystem as a very large, strong team of nature and wildlife. Everything found in the wilderness has a special job to do. While each job may not seem big on its own, it affects several other wildlife species. If one piece of the ecosystem puzzle is missing, all other pieces are affected. Let's take plants, for example. Plants are necessary for survival because they provide food and oxygen. Plants need light from the sun to make food, and animals help spread plant seeds so more plants can grow. When leaves fall, bugs chew at them and help them break down. When leaves break down, they release nutrients into the soil, which new plants can absorb and grow strong and healthy.

Different wildlife species help each other maintain a balanced ecosystem. Bees, for example, pollinate plants so their seeds can spread and more of them can grow. In return for their hard work, plants give bees the nectar they need to make honey. Just like you have everything you need in the human world, wildlife has everything it needs in its ecosystem.

Respecting and Caring for Wildlife

Any interaction you have with wildlife, no matter how small it may seem, can affect its ecosystem and, therefore, harm it. Throwing a plastic bag into a pond, taking a shell home, or picking at plants negatively impacts the ecosystem's health and makes animals more aggressive.

Do you have a pet at home? If not, do you wish to have one? If you get a pet, you will care for it, feed it, and provide it with a safe and comfortable place to live. Wild animals are also living things that need similar things to survive. Earth is not just a human planet. You share it with pets, other animals in the wild, and all living things in nature. It's humans' responsibility to help these animals and avoid harming them and their homes. Therefore, you shouldn't litter or disturb wildlife. Animals have feelings, so you should avoid hurting them and try to help them when they're in trouble.

You should always watch animals from a distance when in the wild, even ones that seem cute and cuddly. You can use binoculars to get a closer look at them, but you should never approach them if you want to stay safe. You should also avoid feeding animals, no matter how hungry they may look. Human food is harmful to wildlife and doesn't contain the nutrients they need. Feeding wild animals regularly will also teach them to rely on you for food. They will no longer find their own meals, which would be a problem if no one else was there to feed them. Feeding animals also makes them less fearful of you, which can put you in danger or encourage them to follow you to unsafe areas, like roads, which can result in their injury.

Hiking Etiquette

Hiking is among the best ways to connect with nature. It is a fun activity that helps you relax and breathe clean, fresh air while exercising. The benefits of hiking are countless. However, you must know a few rules to make the most of your time.

- **Make Way for Climbers**: Climbing up the hill is a lot more work than climbing down. When you're descending, create enough space for those going uphill to pass through.

- **Meeting Bicyclists**: If you plan on cycling, check out the specific park or trail regulations to know whether it's allowed. Bicyclists should generally make way for hikers who are on foot, allowing them to pass first. If you're the one cycling, stop and step to the side whenever you see a hiker. Be mindful of plants and animals, and avoid accidentally hurting them with your bike or feet.

- **Gently Approach Horses**: Whether you're biking or on foot, you should give horses and other similar animals the right of way. Let them pass first. Keep in mind that these animals can get frightened easily, and any sudden movements can put them, those riding them, and even others in danger. Whenever you approach them, use a gentle voice to announce your presence.

- **Say Hello**: Be friendly to other people you encounter on the trail. Say "hello," and let them know you want to pass in a respectful way.

- **Don't Step Off the Trail**: Stay on the rail unless you must let someone else pass. Stepping on something you're not supposed to step on can damage the ecosystem, so be sure to mind where you're standing.

- **Don't Disturb Wildlife**: Use binoculars if you want to take a closer look at animals instead of stepping off the trail and putting them and yourself in danger.

- **Consider Weather Conditions**: Avoid hiking after it has just rained, as muddy and slippery trails are dangerous.

- **Minimize the Noise**: Loud noises on the trail can disturb wildlife and other hikers. Keep your phone on low volume and avoid engaging in loud conversations.

Common Types of Wildlife to Find in the Wilderness

A male deer is easy to identify because of its antlers.
https://unsplash.com/photos/gazelle-under-the-tree-1tsAbBciTic?utm_content=creditShareLink&utm_medium=referral&utm_source=unsplash

- **Deer:** These animals are mostly found in forests and grassland. They vary in size depending on their species and age. Male deer are very easy to identify because they are characterized by their antlers, which grow as they age. Deer are generally active at sunrise and sunset. These animals eat plants and aren't considered dangerous to humans. However, they can display aggressive behavior if they feel threatened. It's best to keep your distance from them.

- **Raccoons:** Raccoons are small to medium-sized furry animals. They are usually grayish to brown in color and have patterns that mimic rings on their tails. They are most active at night and eat both meat and plants. They usually feed on plants, eggs, smaller animals, and insects. Raccoons generally don't attack humans, but they do if they feel threatened. They often carry harmful diseases, so you should keep your distance from them.

- **Skunks:** Skunks are small animals with black fur and white markings down their backs. They are popularly known for their ability to spray bad odors when they feel threatened. Like raccoons, skunks are mostly active at night and eat a wide array of foods. Avoid approaching or provoking skunks, as they might spray you or attack you when startled. Their spraying can be harmful, and the odor is difficult to get rid of.

- **Squirrels:** These small, furry animals come in a variety of colors, including gray, red, and brown. They are mostly active during the day and eat a varied diet, which includes insects, nuts, bird eggs, fruits, and seeds. Respect a squirrel's space and only watch them from a distance. While they are generally harmless, they may resort to biting if they feel scared.

- **Black Bears:** Black bears and brown bears are among the most popular of their species. While black bears grow to be very large, they are still smaller than brown bears. Black bears hibernate during winter and eat a varied diet that includes vegetables, nuts, berries, insects, and meat. You should keep a safe distance from bears at all times. Watch them from afar and make noises to make them aware of your presence.

- **Coyotes:** Coyotes are strong and intelligent medium-sized animals. They have grayish-brown fur and are mostly active during the night. They have a varied diet that ranges from fruit and vegetables to insects, birds, and small mammals. Don't approach coyotes at all, and avoid bringing your pets into areas where they are present. If you must bring a pet along, keep it on a leash beside you.

- **Birds:** Birds are among the most common wildlife you'll find in the wilderness. However, learning how to identify each bird species requires a guide or directory of its own. Each type of bird comes in its own shape, size, and color. Some bird types eat only seeds, some eat worms and other insects, and others eat a variety of both. Sparrows, Bluejays, and Robins are among the most commonly spotted birds. When observing birds, avoid approaching or disturbing them. Simply admire them or use an identification guide to learn more about them from afar.

Safety Precautions for Encountering Wild Animals

Bears

If you encounter a bear, you must communicate that you're a human. No matter how terrified you are, you should keep your voice calm while talking to it. This will allow the bear to identify that you aren't a prey animal. Stay still and wave your arms slowly. Don't be alarmed if the bear moves toward you or stands on its hind legs. This likely means that it's just curious and trying to better understand what you are.

Most bears don't want to attack you.
https://unsplash.com/photos/shallow-focus-photo-of-brown-grizzly-bear-r6w0R6SueQ?utm_content=creditShareLink&utm_medium=referral&utm_source=unsplash

Remind yourself that most bears don't want to attack you. They may growl and engage in other defensive behaviors before they turn away and leave. Continue talking to the bear in a low, calm tone, and avoid screaming or making any sudden movements. You can move away slowly and sideways if the bear doesn't move.

Try not to break away from your group when you're out in the wild. Large groups can intimidate bears. Keep your food stored away, and don't try to escape by climbing up trees, as they'll probably follow you.

Bear attacks are very rare, but it helps to be prepared. If you're attacked by a brown bear, play dead. If it's a black bear, try to escape or fight back. You should also keep bear pepper spray on you.

Coyotes

If a coyote approaches you, keep firmly clapping your hands. Alternate between clapping and swinging your hands all around you to make yourself appear larger than you really are. Through rocks, sticks, and other objects near it to scare it away from you. Keep a whistle or dog spray on you, and avoid running away. If the coyote keeps approaching you, slowly back away into somewhere you can hide.

Snake

If you see a snake, try to remain as calm as you can. The reptile is usually not aggressive unless you provoke it. Observe how it looks so you can identify it later and find out whether it's venomous. Calmly and slowly move away from it while watching it to ensure that it doesn't speed up.

All animals play a significant role in the maintenance of the ecosystem. When visiting wild animals in the wilderness, you must treat them with respect and give them the space they need to perform their daily activities. Otherwise, you'd be putting them and yourself in danger.

Section 6: Creating Useful Tools

Tools are the backbone of civilization. They are one of the main reasons humans are at the top of the food chain. They are used to cook, clean, build, break, make additional tools, and so much more. For your wilderness adventure, you may have already packed a few tools like a compass, a first aid kit, ropes, a topography map, a matchbox, a flashlight, etc.

Did you forget to carry a knife, though? What about a pickaxe or a hammer? How about weapons to defend yourself from possible predators? Even if you did manage to carry all these tools, your backpack must weigh a ton. Why overburden yourself when you can just create any required tool in the wilderness?

Simple Cutting Tools

A knife is a must to create tools out of materials found in nature. Did you forget to pack one? Don't worry. You can create your very own set of cutting tools! All you need is the right type of stone, a thread or a thin rope, and a small wooden stick.

Useful Stone Types

You can't just pick any rock from the ground and start shaping it to make a cutting tool. You will be using the cutting tool to make additional tools, so it should be hard enough and, at the same time, easily shaped into the desired form. Look for the following types of stones to create cutting tools.

- **Flint:** This type of rock is probably the easiest to recognize. It looks like wax but feels like glass. Its outer layer is thin, but it is quite hard inside, making it the perfect stone for molding into a cutting tool. To make sure the stone is indeed flint, strike it against a steel utensil and see if it produces sparks.

Flint is the easiest rock to recognize.
Miguel Calvo, CC BY-SA 4.0 <https://creativecommons.org/licenses/by-sa/4.0>, via Wikimedia Commons: https://commons.wikimedia.org/wiki/File:Silex-Zaragoza.jpg

- **Obsidian:** This is one of the most commonly found rocks in the United States. It's a volcanic rock, so if you are headed to a place with a dormant or extinct volcano, you are bound to find it there. It looks like glass and is dark black in color.

Obsidian is a volcanic rock.
https://commons.wikimedia.org/wiki/File:ObsidianOregon.jpg

- **Jasper:** This has a similar appearance to obsidian, but it occurs in many different colors other than black. It's not as glassy-looking as obsidian.

Jasper occurs in many colors.
https://commons.wikimedia.org/wiki/File:Unpolished_jasper.jpg

- **Felsite:** This rock is defined by its different textures, and its colors can be a variety of black shades. It is also a volcanic rock, so if you cannot find obsidian, you can look for felsite.

Felsite is also a volcanic rock.
https://commons.wikimedia.org/wiki/File:Felsite_-
orbicular_igneous_rock_Guanajuato_Mexico_2530.jpg

Other types of cutting stones include Rhyolite (found near felsite and obsidian) and Quartzite (usually found atop a hill).

How to Make Cutting Tools

Once you have found any of the above rocks, you need to shape them into a stone with sharp edges. If the stone is too big, start off by crushing it into smaller pieces. Pick another rock of the same size. Maintain a safe distance between yourself and the rock to be crushed (at least more than three feet). For added safety, put on biking glasses that cover your eyes entirely, along with riding gloves, thick shoes, a scarf, and full leather clothing.

Then, hurl the rock in your hand at the other rock with sufficient force. If your aim is true, both rocks will be smashed into each other and break apart into small pieces. You will find a readymade sharp-edged stone in the rubble if you are lucky. If not, pick a small piece (flat or elongated) and use the following techniques to create your cutting tool.

- **Percussion:** This technique is primarily shown in survival movies and TV shows. Take two stones, one harder than the other. Hold the softer stone in your palm and strike the hard stone at it with your other hand at an angle (a glancing motion). Tiny flakes from the softer stone will come off. Keep glance striking until a sharp point is produced. You can refine your cutting tool further by striking the other sides of the softer stone to make it into an arrowhead.

- **Bi-Polar Percussion:** This is a relatively safer way of creating a sharp-edged stone. Flakes and shards don't come off randomly here, but the motion is like striking a hammer on a nail, so you need to be very careful. Take a heavy stone with a flat face that can fit in your palm and another smaller, longer, and flatter stone that you want to make into a cutting tool. Hold the smaller stone upright with one hand (grip the middle) on a hard, flat surface, and ram the heavier stone with its flat surface on top of the smaller stone. The latter will be broken into two pieces, both having sharp edges. You can refine the pieces by using the regular percussion technique.

There are many other techniques, like pressure flaking and knapping, but they are much more complicated and are primarily used to refine your tools even further. Coarse tools made from basic percussion techniques are effective enough for now.

Making Cordage

Crafted a good, sharp cutting stone already? Great work! You can't hold it without a grip or a handle, however. Before you go looking for something to attach it to, find something to attach it with. A simple cotton or nylon thread would work. A thin rope would also do the trick. Did you forget to pack either of these things? You can make your very own fastening thread from natural fibers. It is called cordage.

You can use thin strips of bark to fasten your cutting stone to a handle, but there is a high chance that the strips may start thinning and break after heavy use. A cordage is much better and stronger. You will need dry strips of bark from a dead tree or dry strands of dead grass. In live trees, the strips are filled with moisture, so they won't make a strong cordage. Plus, peeling bark off a dead tree is eco-friendly, too.

Remove thin individual strands of fibers from the bark or grass. Follow these steps to make a simple cordage quickly.

1. Place a few individual strands on a flat surface.
2. Bring them together and hold their two ends with your fingers.
3. Roll the entire thing on the surface in a single direction. If you run out of the surface, bring it back and roll it again until the fibers are tightly wound.
4. Hold the middle of your makeshift cordage between your front teeth and stretch the two dangling ends downward with your fingers.
5. Let go of the middle and behold the cordage twisting around itself automatically!

Making a Grip

It is much easier to fashion a grip or a handle than a cordage or a cutting tool. Pick a moderately thick branch that is more or less straight. With your newly made cutting stone, shear the outer skin and cut off any sharp points. If you have sandpaper at hand, you can give a smooth finish to your handiwork.

Then, hold your cutting stone at the top edge of the newly-fashioned grip or handle. The sharp edge should be outward, and a small part of the lower edge should overlap with the grip's top edge. Hold this together with your finger as you wrap your cordage around the intersection. Make sure the wrapping is strong before tying up the loose ends. It mustn't come off after a few good strikes of the cutting tool to a hard surface.

Simple Primitive Weapons and Traps

Wildlife should be preserved, but it doesn't mean you should leave yourself defenseless. You will feel much safer with a spear in your hand and a bow slung on your shoulder. If you are hungry and have no edible plants nearby, a small game trap or a fishing spear will come in handy. You can't expect to use your makeshift simple cutting tool for all the work. (Show a picture of every type of weapon and trap below)

- **Spear**

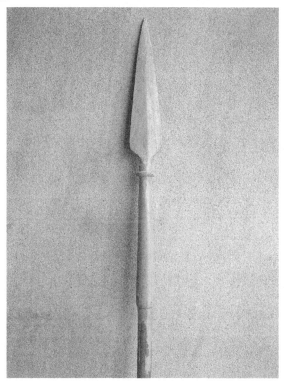

A spear is a longer version of a knife.
Gurnoor ghuman, CC BY-SA 4.0 <https://creativecommons.org/licenses/by-sa/4.0>, via Wikimedia Commons: https://commons.wikimedia.org/wiki/File:Spear_03.jpg

A spear is just a longer version of a knife. The Stone Age people used it to gain a bit of range while hunting. It can also be thrown like a javelin to attack a prey further off. Here's an easy and safe way to fashion a simple spear.

1. Find a long, straight branch from a dead tree (around six feet in length and an inch or two in diameter).

2. Remove the outer skin with your cutting tool, along with any sharp edges.

3. Hold it a few feet away from the edge in one hand, and with the cutting tool in the other hand, carve a sharp tip at the edge of the stick. It's just like sharpening your pencil with a knife.

Alternatively, you can affix an elongated and sharpened stone made from bipolar percussion to the stick with your cordage, the same way you created your cutting tool.

• Fishing Spear

Crafting a fishing spear is harder and more dangerous than a simple spear. Adult supervision is highly recommended. A fishing spear is a long stick with a claw-like opening used to skewer and trap the fish. You will need a thin, sharp knife to make this.

1. Find the same type of branch you did for the simple spear and clear the outer bark and sharp edges with your cutting tool or knife.

2. Use the side edge of the knife to bore through the top of the stick, splitting it in two for just around three to four inches.

3. Pull out the knife and split it again. This time, it is perpendicular to the first split. The structure will seem like four sticks attached to a pole.

4. Wrap a cordage at the base of the splits.

5. Push two small twigs between the splits perpendicular to each other. The twigs should be around half an inch in diameter. This is done to keep the claw open.

6. Tie another cordage around the stick and twigs.

7. Using your cutting tool or knife, sharpen each of the four edges of the claw, and your fishing spear is ready!

Once you learn how to work with the bones below, you can attach the sharpened bones to your spear to make it more effective.

• **Fashioning Bone Tools**

Bones are not only harder than stones but also flexible in nature. They are ideal for crafting hooks, spear points, and needles. They are also readily available in the wilderness from the decayed bodies of long-dead animals. When you find a bone, clean it first in a running stream of water. Alternatively, you can use the bones from the animal or fish you had for lunch.

The safest and easiest way to sharpen a bone is to smash it with a rock. There are bound to be a few sharp points among the debris. These shards are usually supple and can be bent to create a fish hook. Tie your cordage to the other end of the hook and fling it in a lake or a river to catch fish. You can use the harder, sharp-edged bones to replace the stones in your cutting tools and spears.

There are other ways of creating bone tools, like sawing and abrading, but they are highly advanced and unsafe for children.

• **Small Game Trap**

Want to catch animals without getting your hands dirty? The simplest small game trap you can create is a snare. Take your cord and tie a basic knot on one end, keeping an open wide loop. You can lasso the animal or set up a snare trap with the cord hanging from a tree branch. Keep some food near the loop. The animal's head will get stuck in the loop as it tries to pass through. The noose will tighten around its neck when it struggles to pull free. If catching wild animals is forbidden in the area, let the creature loose soon after.

Tool Maintenance and Repair

These makeshift tools created from stones and bones don't usually last long. You will need to sharpen and clean the tools after each use. If you'll be in the wilderness for a couple of days, create at least two cutting tools to maintain the edge of your other tools.

Does the cordage feel loose? Untie and refasten it. Is it fraying, and the thread is coming off? Replace it with fresh cordage. Has the stone point of your spear become small and blunt? Affix another sharp stone there. Make it a habit of maintaining and repairing your tools each morning and evening.

Section 7: First Aid and Emergencies

Whether venturing into the wilderness, embarking on a camping trip, hiking through rugged terrain, or simply enjoying a day at the beach, the great outdoors offers adventure and a connection to nature. However, it also presents inherent risks and challenges that can quickly turn a pleasant outing into an emergency. That's where the significance of first aid skills becomes evident.

With its unpredictable environments, wildlife encounters, and remote locations, the wilderness lacks immediate access to medical facilities and professional assistance. In these scenarios, your knowledge of first aid means the difference between a manageable incident and a life-threatening emergency.

Here are several key reasons why learning first aid skills is necessary for children, especially in the wilderness.

Rapid Response to Injuries

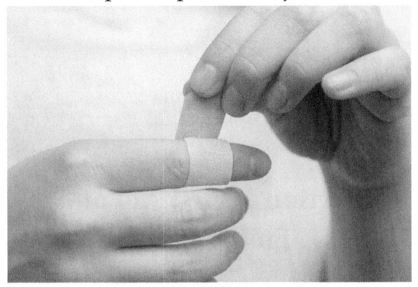

First aid knowledge can allow you to respond quickly.
https://unsplash.com/photos/person-with-band-aid-on-middle-finger-SwWjCbIIoFE?utm_content=creditShareLink&utm_medium=referral&utm_source=unsplash

Accidents can happen in the blink of an eye – a fall, a burn, or a deep cut from a sharp object. First aid knowledge allows you to respond quickly, promptly addressing wounds, fractures, and other injuries, reducing the risk of complications and infections.

Saving Lives

In remote outdoor settings, it can take a long time for professional help to arrive. Learning first aid can save a life in dire situations, such as when someone is suffering from a heart attack, severe allergic reaction, or a near-drowning incident.

Alleviating Discomfort

Minor injuries like sprains, insect stings, and sunburns can disrupt an outdoor experience. First aid skills enable you to provide relief so you can continue your adventure rather than having to cut it short due to discomfort.

Enhancing Preparedness

Being well-prepared for outdoor activities means more than just packing the right gear. It's knowing how to use that gear and adapt to unexpected challenges. First aid skills provide you with the tools to stay calm, assess situations, and respond effectively, even in high-stress situations.

Encouraging Responsible Recreation

Having first aid knowledge promotes responsible outdoor recreation. It encourages individuals to respect the environment, leave no trace, and be more considerate of their fellow outdoor enthusiasts, contributing to the overall well-being of natural spaces.

Whether you've been on many outdoor adventures or are just starting to explore nature, these skills are essential.

Basic Wilderness First Aid Kit

Assembling a basic wilderness first aid kit is crucial for outdoor activities, as it ensures that you have the necessary supplies to address common injuries and emergencies while keeping the kit compact and portable. Begin with a durable, waterproof container to store your first aid supplies. Options include zip-lock bags, small waterproof pouches, or dedicated first-aid kits available in outdoor stores.

List of Items to Include

- **Sterile Gauze Pads:** These are used for cleaning and covering wounds.
- **Adhesive Bandages:** Use them to protect small cuts and blisters.
- **Adhesive Tape:** Helps secure dressings and immobilize injured areas.
- **Antiseptic Wipes or Solutions:** These are crucial for cleaning wounds and preventing infection.
- **Tweezers:** Handy for removing splinters or debris from wounds.
- **Pain Relievers (e.g., Acetaminophen or Ibuprofen):** Helpful for minor aches and pains.
- **Antihistamines (e.g., Benadryl):** Useful for treating allergic reactions to insect stings, food, or plants.
- **Sunscreen:** Protect your skin from harmful UV rays, especially on sunny days. You can also add a lip balm to prevent chapped lips and sunburn.
- **Insect Repellent:** Keeps mosquitoes and other bugs away.

- **Skin Protection:** Calamine lotion or hydrocortisone cream: Treat skin irritations and bug bites.
- **Wound Care Bandages:** Steri-strips or butterfly bandages: Use for closing small wounds.
- **Scissors:** Small scissors or a multi-tool with scissors: Handy for cutting tape and clothing.
- **Whistle:** Use to signal for help in an emergency.
- **Documentation:** A copy of your personal identification, medical history, and any relevant contact numbers. This information is vital for medical professionals in case of severe emergencies.
- **Manual:** A basic first aid manual of instructions for common wilderness injuries.
- **Personal Supplies:** Any personal items specific to your needs, such as extra prescription medications, medical bracelets, or other condition-specific supplies.

After completing the items checklist, review the contents again and ensure your first aid kit is compact, lightweight, and easily accessible. Avoid filling the kit with too many disposable items or medications, as it will only make your kit heavier. For example, you may need a few tablets for each medication instead of carrying the entire pack. Likewise, a pair or two of gloves will suffice instead of packing a dozen in your first-aid kit.

You should be able to attach it to your backpack or belt using carabiners or straps or keep it in an outer pocket. Make sure everyone in your group knows where the kit is and how to use its contents. Regularly inspect your first aid kit, replacing damaged, expired, or used items. Having the supplies is not enough; you must learn how to use them correctly.

Evaluating the Severity of Injury

Assessing the severity of injuries and prioritizing care, especially for life-threatening injuries, is a critical skill when faced with an emergency outdoors. You must stay calm and assess the situation to provide effective and timely first aid. Here's a step-by-step guide on how to do this:

Maintain Your Composure

First and foremost, stay calm. Panic affects your ability to provide appropriate care. Take a few deep breaths to help you focus.

Ensure Your Safety

Before rushing to help others, evaluate the scene for potential hazards, such as falling rocks, unstable terrain, or dangerous wildlife. Move to a safe location if necessary.

Call for Help

If you have access to communication (cell phone or radio), call for emergency assistance immediately. In remote areas, a satellite communication device is a lifesaver.

Assess Responsiveness

Gently tap or shake the injured person and ask if they are okay. Determine their level of consciousness and responsiveness.

Check for Breathing

If the person is unresponsive, check for breathing. Place your ear near their mouth and nose while looking at their chest for any rise and fall. If they are not breathing or are breathing abnormally, begin CPR if you are trained to do so.

Survey for Life-Threatening Bleeding

Look for life-threatening bleeding, which can be arterial and lead to severe blood loss. Apply pressure to the wound with a sterile bandage (if available) or any clean cloth. If the bleeding is profuse and doesn't stop, consider applying a tourniquet above the wound if you know how to do this correctly.

Assess for Shock

Check for signs of shock, which can occur with severe injuries. Symptoms include rapid, shallow breathing, confusion, paleness, and cold, clammy skin. If shock is suspected, keep the injured person warm, elevate their legs slightly, and reassure them.

Airway Management

If the person is conscious but has difficulty breathing due to an obstruction, perform first aid measures to clear the airway. This could include the Heimlich maneuver for choking. (If you don't know how to perform this maneuver, ask an adult to show you!)

Continue Assessment

Assess the injured person for other injuries or medical conditions. Prioritize care based on the severity of these issues. For example, a head injury, a compromised airway, or a spinal injury should be addressed as soon as a priority over less severe injuries. Continue to monitor the injured person's condition and adjust your care as needed. Remember, conditions can change, so regularly check on the injured person.

Comfort and Reassure

Throughout the process, provide emotional support and reassurance to the injured person. Keeping them calm can have a positive impact on their recovery.

Remember that staying calm and organized in your approach is essential in any emergency. Assess the situation, identify life-threatening injuries, and provide immediate care as needed while waiting for professional help to arrive. Your ability to prioritize and provide care can make a significant difference in the outcome of an emergency in the wilderness.

Treating Minor Wounds

1. Ensure the area is safe and free from hazards.
2. Wash your hands or use hand sanitizer if water is unavailable.
3. Examine the wound for its size, depth, and cleanliness. If it's a minor cut or scrape, proceed.
4. Clean the wound.
5. Rinse the wound gently with clean water to remove dirt and debris.
6. If available, use an antiseptic wipe or solution to clean the wound.
7. Pat the area dry with a clean cloth or sterile gauze.
8. Apply an Antibiotic Ointment: If you have antibiotic ointment, apply a thin layer to prevent infection.
9. Place a sterile adhesive bandage or dressing over the wound.
10. Change the bandage daily and keep the wound clean.
11. Over-the-counter pain relievers can help manage discomfort.

Treating Strains

1. Encourage the individual to rest and avoid using the injured area.
2. Apply an ice pack wrapped in a cloth to reduce swelling and pain. However, if you have trouble finding ice in your surroundings, use water from a nearby stream or lake, dip a clean cloth in it, and compress the injured area.
3. Use an elastic bandage to provide support.
4. Elevate the injured area above heart level to minimize swelling.

Over-the-counter pain relievers can help manage pain and inflammation—allow time for the strain to heal. Seek medical attention if the pain or swelling worsens or doesn't improve.

Treating Burns

1. Ensure there is no ongoing risk of burn (e.g., remove the person from the heat source).
2. Run cold water over the burn for about 10-20 minutes or until the pain subsides.
3. If there are blisters, leave them intact to prevent infection.
4. If available, apply an over-the-counter burn ointment.
5. Use a sterile, non-stick dressing or a clean cloth to cover the burn.

First Aid for Snakebites

1. Panic can worsen the situation. Encourage the person to keep the bitten limb as still as possible.
2. Remove any tight clothing, jewelry, or accessories near the bite site that could constrict blood flow if swelling occurs.
3. If possible, keep the affected limb slightly elevated to reduce swelling.
4. Call for emergency help and get to the nearest medical facility as soon as possible.
5. Note the time of the bite.

First Aid for Stings

1. If a stinger is present (as in bee or wasp stings), gently scrape it off with a flat-edged object like a credit card.
2. Clean the sting site with soap and water.
3. Use a cold pack to reduce pain and swelling.

Infection Prevention

4. Wash wounds regularly with soap and water.
5. Keep dressings clean and dry. Change them daily.
6. Picking at scabs can increase the risk of infection.
7. Watch for redness, increasing pain, pus, or fever. Seek medical attention if these signs appear.

Seeking Medical Attention

In case of burns or strains, try seeking immediate medical attention. For snake bites, even a non-venomous snake, seek medical attention for wound care and tetanus prevention. For allergic reactions, if the injured person shows signs of a severe allergic reaction, such as difficulty breathing or swelling of the face, lips, or tongue, call 911 or emergency services.

In all cases, if there's any doubt or concern about the severity of the injury, it's best to seek professional medical help. Prompt medical attention can prevent complications and ensure the best possible outcome for the injured person.

Using Whistles and Signaling Devices

A whistle can help you call for help.
https://www.pexels.com/photo/hand-holding-a-whistle-7207354/

- Make sure you carry a whistle when you're out in the wilderness. Whistles are like your superpower for calling for help.
- Learn this special whistle code: three quick, short blasts, then pause and do it again. It's the secret signal to tell others you need help.
- If you need to use your whistle, find a place with lots of room where people can see and hear you. It's easier for your signal to travel in wide-open areas.
- When you blow your whistle, do it with enough force so the sound travels far, but don't exhaust yourself. A short, strong blow is perfect.
- If you're in trouble, blow your whistle three times, pause, and do it again. Keep doing this until help arrives or someone answers.
- Besides whistles, you can also use signal mirrors, flashlights, or anything colorful that stands out. Make sure you know how to use them, too.

When to Signal for Help

- Suppose something really scary happens, like a bad injury, getting lost, or coming across a dangerous animal. In that case, it's time to use your whistle.
- If you're too tired or something else makes it impossible to continue what you were doing, blow your whistle for help.
- If you're not prepared for the weather conditions, like a storm or extreme heat, use your whistle to call for help.

Seeking Adult Help for Serious Emergencies

- Remember, while you're learning cool first aid and survival skills, the real heroes are the grown-ups. If something *really bad* happens, don't be shy – get an adult right away.
- If you have a phone or a radio, use it to talk to the grown-ups in your group. Tell them what's happening, and they'll know what to do. They can call for professional help, like park rangers or doctors.
- Make sure you know important numbers, like 911. That's the fastest way to reach the right grown-ups when things get tough.

By using your whistle and other signaling devices wisely and calling in the grown-ups when there's a big emergency, you'll be all set for safe and fun outdoor adventures.

Section 8: Finding Your Way

In this chapter, you will learn navigational skills to help you explore the wilderness and find your way back to safety in emergencies. This chapter explains what cardinal directions are and why they're useful. It also teaches you how to read a map and use natural cues like the sun, stars, and shadows to find directions. You'll also find tips on marking trails and paths to trace your way back to safety or help rescuers find you in case of emergencies.

What Are Cardinal Directions?

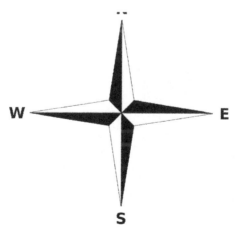

The cardinal directions.

Directions are methods of communication that help people explain and understand what things are in relation to others. An example of giving directions would be saying that the coffee shop is on the left side of the restaurant. However, this can be very confusing if you aren't facing the restaurant. This is where cardinal directions come in.

Cardinal directions give accurate geographic directions as they don't depend on the direction you're facing. North, South, East, and West are the main cardinal directions in geography. If you're facing a map, the north will refer to the upper part of the map, the south will refer to the lower one, the west will refer to where your left hand is holding the map, and the east will be where your right hand is.

For instance, if someone says, "The coffee shop is found west of the restaurant," you won't have to face a certain way to get there correctly. West will always be west regardless of where you're standing. If you know which states are on the map, you can easily tell which part of the USA you're in and which direction you need to go to get to another state.

For instance, if you want to travel from Wyoming, which is in North America, to New Mexico, you would have to travel south. If you want to go from California, which is located in the west, to Utah, you would have to travel east. You can use a compass or a map to know where you're located and which direction you need to head in. You can also use natural cues like the sun and the stars to know where to go.

How to Read a Map

Maps are considered one of the easiest ways to navigate.

Maps are considered one of the easiest ways to navigate and understand geographical information. A map gives you a bird's view of the area and presents all the necessary information.

Step 1: Read the Title

Reading the map's title is the first and most important step in reading a map. There are many different types of maps. There are maps of the Earth, which tell you where each country is located. There is a map for each country, which includes the location of every city and other geographic features like mountains, deserts, forests, and rivers. There are maps of each city and even town that tell you how to get to certain shops, malls, parks, restaurants, and so on.

Some maps illustrate significant routes in history, such as a map of the Silk Road, one of the most important trade routes. It shows the key locations of the trade route, where it started and connected to, various branches of the routes, and how traders could choose between different paths. There are also maps illustrating the migration patterns of certain animals at different times of the year.

Reading the title helps you determine if this is the map you need. If you're in Milan, Italy, a map of a different city, such as Firenze, wouldn't help. You should also pay attention to the date on which the map was created. You should use recent maps to ensure that they're up to date. You don't want to use a map to get to a restaurant only to discover that this map was created in 1958 and that a hair salon has taken its place.

Step 2: Know Its Orientation

To use a map correctly, you should know where each cardinal direction lies on the map. You don't want to hold it upside down accidentally. Fortunately, most maps have a small illustration of a compass that is labeled N (north), S (south), E (east), and W (west), allowing you to orient the map correctly.

Step 3: Know Its Scale

Maps are accurate yet scaled-down representations of certain areas and movements. A map that is true to size would be very impractical. A map is similar to what it would look like if you took a very high-quality picture of an entire country and printed it onto paper. The picture would show the exact location of everything in the country, but in a much smaller size than it really is. Knowing the scale of the map means knowing the real distance between locations. When using a map to navigate, this is the only way you'll know how far you need to travel to get to your target area.

Step 4: Use the Map's Key

Most maps have a key or a legend that tells you what different illustrations on the map mean. Map makers use different shapes, symbols, colors, and forms of lines and arrows to communicate different things. For instance, a blue square could mean a lake, a blue line could mean a river, a tree may refer to a park, and a dashed line could represent mountains.

Remember that there isn't one key or legend that all maps stick to. Therefore, you should refer to the specific legend offered on the map you're using.

Step 5: Determine the Borders

After you've learned the basics of reading a map, you need to determine where the place you're searching for is in real life. To do that, you need to understand that some maps use a standard grid pattern, which means that it's divided into many small equal squares based on the latitude and longitude. The latitude is an imaginary line that runs vertically down the Earth, from the North Pole to the South Pole, while the longitude is an imaginary line that runs across the Earth vertically. It is located halfway between the North and South Poles.

The longitude and latitude help with navigation and mapping. Even today's GPS apps and devices use longitude and latitude to function correctly. They are also used to identify locations on the map and help with weather forecasting.

The grid can either be visible or invisible on the map. Dividing the map into squares helps you determine exactly where places lie. Other maps, especially if they represent smaller areas, such as cities, may use their own system or code consisting of numbers and letters. This code helps map readers find places in real life. The code usually tells you which line to follow up and down, according to the longitude, and which line to follow side to side, according to the latitude.

Finding Directions Using the Sun and the Stars

Finding Directions in the Morning

The sun helps you locate the north, which can help you find all the other directions. You'll only need a relatively straight stick that is around 1 meter long.

1. Find a place that is bush-free and push the stick into the ground. It's okay if the stick leans a little. The most important thing is that you're able to see a clear shadow of it on the ground.

2. Use a stone or any small tool to mark the stick's shadow on the ground.

3. Wait for 10 to 15 minutes until the stick's shadow has moved, and use another tool to mark the new shadow.

4. Use your finger or another stick to draw a straight line, connecting the first and second rocks or markings together. Continue drawing the line about a foot past the second marking.

5. Stand facing the shadows, with your left toe at the first marking and your right toe at the end of the line you just drew. You are now facing the true north.

6. You can easily find the other directions now that you're facing north.

7. Draw a line across the line you drew, creating a cross. Mark the directions on it.

Finding Directions at Night

If you're in the northern hemisphere, these instructions will help you.

The Big Dipper can help you find the North Star.

The Big Dipper is a group or constellation of seven stars that can help you determine where the North Star is. The Big Dipper looks like a line connecting to the bowl. The two stars at the end of the bowl are called pointers. You will find the North Star if you trace a straight line out from the pointers. The Big Dipper slowly rotates around the North Star, constantly changing its location. However, if you trace a straight line from the pointers, it'll lead to the North Star.

You can also use Cassiopeia, a constellation of five stars, to locate the North Star. This constellation resembles the letter "M" a little. Draw an imaginary line down the letter, extending it from the part where it opens. The straight line should connect to the North Star.

If you're in the southern hemisphere

Find the Southern Cross, a constellation of four stars that looks like a tilted cross, to determine the direction of the south. The two stars that create the longer line in the cross are called pointers. Extend a line from the end of the cross (around five times longer than its length). From this point, draw a line downward and choose a landmark, such as a mountain range, to mark the direction of the south.

Use Trail Markers

Marking the trail as you go along helps you avoid getting lost. You can always trace your steps back by following your markings. Trail markers are also important for your safety because they help rescuers find you in an emergency.

- Most people use chalk to mark key locations on the journey. You can use symbols that mean different things or write short messages for yourself. Chalk is one of the best ways to mark your trail without harming the environment, as it usually washes off after a couple of days.

- Chalk might not be suitable if the weather is damp or rainy. In this case, you should consider using environmental materials like rock cairns, stones, sticks, and pine cones. You can also paint marks on trees or place ribbons, but these options may not be suitable if you're walking along private property or in national parks.

Now you know the basics of navigation and wayfinding. You know how to read a map, a skill most people don't know how to do! You can navigate your way around cities without relying on GPS and can determine the cardinal directions by using only the sun and the stars. Besides being valuable knowledge, this is very cool information to have!

Section 9: Additional Survival Hacks

In this section, you will find several tips, hacks, and advice on enhancing your wilderness and survival skills. With this additional knowledge, you will thrive in the great outdoors. You will learn how to mentally, physically, and emotionally deal with emergencies and safely observe the wildlife. You will also learn about a few multi-purpose household tools you should consider packing.

Emergency Signaling

Learning how to signal for emergencies is among the most vital survival skills. Things can go wrong even when you least expect them to. You might lose your group, find yourself in severe weather conditions that are difficult to navigate through, get injured, fall ill, or become extremely exhausted and dehydrated. Being in the wild, where there isn't any mobile signal or internet, requires you to learn other methods to ask others for help.

S.O.S.

S.O.S. stands for "save our souls" or "save our ship." It is the most popular signal, as people worldwide understand it's a call for help. Morse code S.O.S. is a pattern consisting of three dots, three dashes, and three dots "...---...". The Morse code was used to communicate important messages through electric currents during World War 2.

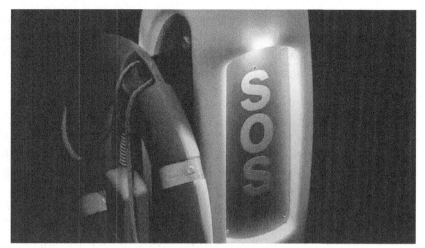

S.O.S. stands for "Save Our Souls."
https://www.pexels.com/photo/red-lifebuoy-in-close-up-shot-9658885/

This signal can be done through either sound or light. You can use a pipe or any other strong material and bang it on a hard surface to do this code "...--..." in the form of sound. Ask your parents to help you look up what the S.O.S. Morse Code sounds like and the right way to do it. Learn and practice it in case you ever need to do it.

Using a flashlight is another way to use the S.O.S. Morse Code. To do it, you'll turn your flashlight on and off quickly three times, then turn it on and hold for a few seconds before turning it back off three times, and then turn it on and off quickly three more times. You can also look up how to do the S.O.S. signal using a flashlight on YouTube. This method, of course, works best at night. You can direct your flashlight at a passing airplane.

If you have a hunter in your group, ask them to fire three shots in the air to signal the need for help. If you have a car, you can honk and flash the headlights in patterns of three. Packing two-way radios and agreeing on a certain frequency to communicate on is a great idea. This way, lost individuals can press the transmit button in patterns of three to signal distress. However, always have a backup plan as these radios only work within a certain range of communication.

Reflected Sunlight

If you need to call for help in the morning, use a mirror to reflect sunlight. You can buy specialized mirrors at a camping store or use any reflective surface. Use your fingers to create a "V" or peace sign at the target you want help from. Keep moving the mirror with your other hand until you find the position that allows the reflection of the sunlight to face the target. Do this in patterns of three to show that you need help. You should never flash signals at airplanes unless you are in an actual emergency.

Build a Fire

After finding water, food, and shelter, learning to build a fire is the most important survival skill. You need fire to stay warm when the temperature drops, scare off some potentially dangerous wild animals, and, of course, have a source of light. If an emergency happens during the day, you can put grass, rubber tires, or green vegetation on your fire to make more smoke without putting it out. Be careful not to let the fire get out of control. At night, create three fires that take the shape of a triangle. Avoid building the fire among the trees or in a hidden area so people can see it clearly.

Use Bright Colors

Use any brightly-colored item that doesn't blend in with the environment to attract people's attention. Use clothes, blankets, sleeping bags, and any other materials to spell out large words like "S.O.S." or "HELP" on the ground. Each letter should be around 12 feet long. If you don't have that many items to use, you can stomp the words into the snow or use a stick to dig the words into the sand. You can even arrange rocks to spell the words out on the ground. Make sure, however, to put some colored items into trees around the area so your call for help can be seen. You can also create a flag with a red cloth attached to the end of the longest stick you can find and wave it to any plane or other passersby.

Glowing Light Stick

Swinging a glowing light stick to create the shape of a circle can grab the attention of potential helpers. Put a string through one end of a chemical light stick and swing it around to create a huge luminant circle. Keep in mind that these sticks can only be lit up once, but they usually last for around 8 to 12 hours.

Observing Wildlife

Nothing is worse than going on a trip in the wild, expecting to see many amazing creatures, but leaving without seeing any! You need to do some things to ensure a successful wildlife observation trip without putting yourself or the animals in danger.

Consider the Location and Time

To avoid disappointment, don't expect to see animals that aren't where you'll be. Research which animals live in the area you'll be visiting. Find out what they look like, learn about their behaviors, read about safety concerns regarding the animal, and know when they're most active. Also, consider the time of year you'll be visiting, as some animals hibernate during winter.

Start Exploring Early

Most animals are active either early in the morning or in the evening. Wake up early to start exploring and observe animals in the daylight. You may not find many animals in the afternoon when it's generally sunny and dry.

Stay Quiet and Attentive

Animals can sense your presence before you even realize you're there. In most cases, they'll flee to protect themselves, and you won't get to see them. So, be very quiet when observing in the wild, keep your cell phone on silent, and avoid talking to others. Be careful not to step on twigs or leaves or bump into anything to avoid making noise. Listen attentively to any movements in your surroundings to easily spot animals and determine their presence.

Consider the Wind and Smell

Most animals have a very sharp sense of smell. They can pick up on even the slightest odors from miles away. Believe it or not, some animals' sense of smell is much stronger than their eyesight! They will likely smell you before they can see you, so avoid spraying perfume on, applying scented body lotions, or using and carrying other scented items. Try to move against the direction of the wind so your scent doesn't get carried over.

Blend In

Blend in with the surrounding environment and avoid wearing bright colors. If you're in the forest, wear earthy tones like brown and green. If it's snowy, dress in white or light colors.

Find a Good Spot and Wait

Find a good spot and wait from a distance. Waiting for animals to pass by can feel extremely boring. However, remember that you'll see more animals if you wait and stay still rather than actively searching for wildlife.

Survival Psychology

Survival psychology refers to the mental and emotional attitudes you need to survive challenging situations in the wilderness. Practicing survival psychology helps you keep calm and focus when things get tough, allowing you to make quick and smart decisions. It is key to managing your fear and staying composed to do the right thing.

For instance, if you see a bear, it is generally recommended that you stay still and quiet. However, someone who goes into panic mode might end up screaming and running, which may trigger an attack. If you get lost, do your best to stay calm so you can create emergency signals with the resources you have. On the other hand, someone who feels panicked won't be able to think clearly and come up with practical solutions.

Start by taking a few deep breaths when you're in a challenging situation. This helps put your mind at ease and decrease worry. Breathe in slowly on 4 counts, hold your breath for 4 counts, and breathe out on 4 counts. Breathe normally for another 4 counts, and repeat until you feel calmer. Maintaining a positive mindset is also crucial when you're in trouble. You have to remind yourself that rescue and survival are possible.

If you're lost, think about everything you need to do to survive, such as finding shelter, food, and water. Tackle the list of things in order of most to least important. Remember that resting and taking a half-hour break when you feel exhausted before resuming your plan is fine.

Additional Survival Tools

The following are some household tools that can help you survive in the wilderness:

Large, Durable Garbage Bags

Large, durable, high-quality garbage bags can be used to store items safely or even create a shelter in times of emergencies. You can use heavy-duty garbage bags to make clothing articles, waterproof beds, or raincoats. You can also use garbage bags to collect or store water when you're running out.

Hand Sanitizer

If you're out in the wild, you probably have limited to no access to water and soap. Using hand sanitizer regularly will help you stay clean and hygienic and avoid illnesses and diseases.

Duct Tape

Duct tape can help secure your shelter, make it waterproof, repair broken items, and patch up ruined clothes.

Chapstick

Even though Chapstick is mainly used for cosmetic purposes, this tool is indispensable in the wilderness. Chapstick can stop wounds from bleeding, ease sunburn, and even serve as candles.

Aluminum Foil

Foil can be used in many ways.
https://unsplash.com/photos/grayscale-photo-of-leaves-on-ground-wpOnFM9hjNI?utm_content=creditShareLink&utm_medium=referral&utm_source=unsplash

You can use aluminum foil to collect water, create plates and bowls, and even make frying pans. This material is also useful for emergency signaling, as it's highly reflective. You can start fires using aluminum foil and AA batteries, as well.

Now you know what to do in case of emergencies when you're out in the wilderness. You should be able to devise a solid plan of action if you get lost or injured and know which items to pack to make life easier out in the wild.

Thank You Message

"May your trails be crooked, winding, lonesome, dangerous, leading to the most amazing view. May your mountains rise into and above the clouds."

Edward Abbey

Taking an interest in a new skill and investing time to read and learn about it is an admirable habit. You should be proud of yourself for coming this far. While the main point of spending time in the wild is stepping out of your comfort zone, connecting with nature, and doing all sorts of exciting and fun activities, you have to remain mindful of your surroundings. The priority is to stay safe and sound while still enjoying yourself.

Your journey doesn't end with these pages, as there are so many more tips and tricks you can explore to enhance and add to your camping experience.

As important as it is to learn what to do in certain situations, you must remember that practice makes perfect, and words are not a substitute for trial and expertise.

Camping is a magical experience that builds character and allows you to explore parts of yourself you didn't know existed. Nature is a good teacher regarding resilience, endurance, and patience. Remember that it's also a great opportunity to bond and forge stronger connections with the people you care about through common experiences and lasting memories.

The skills you'll learn from your exposure to the wilderness will not only serve you in the outdoors. The more you learn how to depend on yourself and survive in challenging circumstances, the more confidence you'll gain. You'll find that your self-worth rises and is reflected in every other aspect of your life. You'll see noticeable positive changes in your physical and mental health.

The best way to learn about the wilderness is by trying, jumping right into the fire, and foraging for yourself on the narrow terrains of the forest.

As you delve more into the natural world, you'll feel more at home and more in sync with Mother Nature. No homework, no exams, no stress, just you and the open green road, free to be yourself without any judgment.

Here's another book by Dion Rosser that you might like

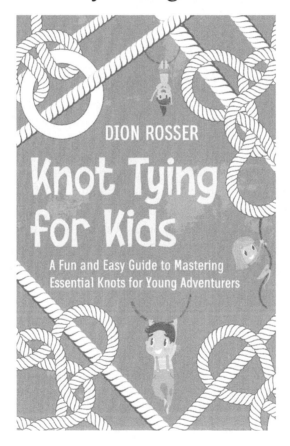

References

A beginner's guide to wilderness and backcountry hiking prep. (2015, July 23). National Park Foundation; #creator. https://www.nationalparks.org/connect/blog/beginners-guide-wilderness-backcountry-hiking-prep

Low, R. (2022, November 16). How to plan a multi-day outdoor adventure. Adventure Treks. https://www.adventuretreks.com/blog/multi-day-adventure/

Mentor, C. (2020, March 25). 5 basic survival skills. Wilderness Awareness School. https://wildernessawareness.org/articles/5-basic-survival-skills/

Pinkston, J. (2021, January 5). Teaching Kids Survival Skills. Don't Die In The Woods. https://dontdieinthewoods.com/blogs/survival-skills/teaching-kids-survival-skills

Pisner, J. (2020, November 11). 13 steps to plan a backpacking trip. Backhacker Babe. https://www.backhackerbabe.com/blog/13-steps-to-plan-a-backpacking-trip

Skurka, A. (2020, July 8). How to plan a successful backpacking trip in 7 steps. Outside Online. https://www.outsideonline.com/outdoor-adventure/hiking-and-backpacking/how-to-plan-backpacking-trip/

Steinberg, B. (2021, January 28). A guide to safe & effective planning for trips into the wilderness. Silent Sports. https://silentsportsmagazine.com/2021/01/28/a-guide-to-safe-effective-planning-for-trips-into-the-wilderness/

(N.d.-a). Rei.com. https://www.rei.com/learn/expert-advice/backpack-planning.html

(N.d.-b). Veggievagabonds.com. https://veggievagabonds.com/adventure-planning/

Anderberg, J. (2016, April 20). How to find water in the wild. The Art of Manliness; Art of Manliness. https://www.artofmanliness.com/skills/outdoor-survival/how-to-find-water-in-the-wild/

Bennett, J. (2016, December 8). Everything you need to know about foraging for food in the wild. Popular Mechanics. https://www.popularmechanics.com/adventure/outdoors/tips/a24203/eat-forage-food-wild-alone-history-channel/

Bryant, C. W. (2021, April 9). How to find water in the wild. MapQuest Travel. https://www.mapquest.com/travel/survival/wilderness/how-to-find-water.htm

Dandelions for your salad. (n.d.). Eatright.org. https://www.eatright.org/food/food-groups/vegetables/dandelions-for-your-salad

DNews. (2011, November 4). Top ways to purify water in the wilderness. Seeker. https://www.seeker.com/top-ways-to-purify-water-in-the-wilderness-1765491027.html

Foraging for wild edibles: A practical approach. (n.d.). Alderleaf Wilderness College. https://www.wildernesscollege.com/foraging-for-wild-edibles.html

How to find water in the wilderness. (2018, October 19). Bushcraft Buddy. https://bushcraftbuddy.com/how-to-find-water-in-the-wilderness/

Jones, B. (2018, August 3). A beginner's guide to finding wild edible plants that won't kill you. Popular Science. https://www.popsci.com/find-wild-edible-plants/

Naranjo, N. (2023, May 12). A camper's guide to water containers and safe drinking solutions. LuminAID. https://luminaid.com/blogs/news/camping-water-containers

Schauf, C. (2018, September 27). How to purify water in the wild. Uncharted Supply Company. https://unchartedsupplyco.com/blogs/news/purify-water-in-wild

Seitz, D. (2020, February 5). How to find drinkable water in the wild. Popular Science. https://www.popsci.com/story/diy/find-drinkable-water-wild/

Two ways to purify water (U.S. National Park service). (n.d.). Nps.gov. https://www.nps.gov/articles/2wayspurifywater.htm

Williams, T. (2023, June 27). Your Survival Guide on how to find Water in the Wilderness. Desert Island Survival. https://www.desertislandsurvival.com/how-to-find-water/

(N.d.-a). Masterclass.com. https://www.masterclass.com/articles/universal-edibility-test

(N.d.-b). Masterclass.com. https://www.masterclass.com/articles/foraging-guide

(N.d.-c). Masterclass.com. https://www.masterclass.com/articles/how-to-find-water

3 things a fire needs - frontier fire protection. (n.d.). Frontierfireprotection.com. https://www.frontierfireprotection.com/3-things-fire-needs/

5 precautions to keep your bonfire or campfire safe. (2016, September 28). Fbfs.com. https://www.fbfs.com/learning-center/5-precautions-to-keep-your-bonfire-or-campfire-safe

Crew, C. (2021, October 12). How to make a campfire and leave no trace. Campsited. https://www.campsited.com/en/blog/how-to-make-a-campfire-and-leave-no-trace/

Edelen, B. (2007, December 19). 6 ways to make fire without matches or a lighter. WikiHow. https://www.wikihow.com/Make-Fire-Without-Matches-or-a-Lighter

Forest Survival Information. (2021, July 5). How to find dry firewood. Forest Info. https://forestinfo.org/how-to-find-dry-firewood/

Lean-to fire - the best way to build A campfire? (n.d.). Firewood For Life. https://www.firewood-for-life.com/lean-to-fire.html

Log Cabin Fire. (n.d.). Firewood For Life. https://www.firewood-for-life.com/log-cabin-fire.html

London, S. (2013, April 25). Back to basics with the fire triangle. Scutum London. https://www.scutumlondon.co.uk/help-advice/basics-fire-triangle/

Outdoor skills: Teaching kids how to build A fire & fire safety tips. (2021, March 8). RUN WILD MY CHILD. https://runwildmychild.com/building-fires-kids/

Teepee Fire. (n.d.). Firewood For Life. https://www.firewood-for-life.com/teepee-fire.html

Top 10 tips for campfire safety. (n.d.). Reserveamerica.com. https://www.reserveamerica.com/articles/camping/top-10-tips-for-campfire-safety

Barber, B. (2023, March 17). 7 most important tarp knots to know. Mom Goes Camping. https://momgoescamping.com/tarp-knots/

Higgins, D. (n.d.). How to build a shelter. Youngnaturalistsclub.com. http://youngnaturalistsclub.com/2020/05/15/how-to-build-a-shelter/

Master, F. (2023, May 12). The silent threat: 5 tips on how to identify A dead tree. Forest Master. https://forest-master.com/2023/05/12/5-tips-on-how-to-identify-a-dead-tree/

Survival skills challenge: Building a shelter. (2017, July 31). There's Just One Mommy. https://theresjustonemommy.com/survival-skills-challenge-building-a-shelter/

(N.d.). Blm.gov. https://www.blm.gov/sites/default/files/documents/files/Learn_CCSC_Nature-Learning-Downloads_Shelter-Building.pdf

Buchholz, R. (2021, May 3). How to get kids to respect wildlife. Family. https://www.nationalgeographic.com/family/article/respect-wildlife

Common Raccoon (Procyon lotor). (n.d.). https://tpwd.texas.gov/huntwild/wild/species/raccoon/

Coyote: Mammals: Species Information: Wildlife: Fish & Wildlife: Maine Dept of Inland Fisheries and Wildlife. (n.d.). https://www.maine.gov/ifw/fish-wildlife/wildlife/species-information/mammals/coyote.html

Dragoo, J. (2023, October 3). Skunk | Scent, Size, Habitat, & Facts. Encyclopedia Britannica. https://www.britannica.com/animal/skunk

Hiking Etiquette (U.S. National Park Service). (n.d.). https://www.nps.gov/articles/hikingetiquette.htm

Information on Common Wildlife Species | Westford, MA. (n.d.). https://westfordma.gov/151/Information-on-Common-Wildlife-Species

Leave No Trace. (2023, July 2). Principle 6: Respect Wildlife - Leave No Trace. https://lnt.org/why/7-principles/respect-wildlife/

Leave No Trace - Respect Wildlife. (n.d.). https://www.leavenotracedude.com/respect-wildlife.php

Oceans2Earth, & Oceans2Earth. (2022). Why we need to show animals kindness and respect. Oceans2Earth. https://oceans2earth.org/why-we-need-to-show-animals-kindness-and-respect/

Squirrels 101: Facts, Photos & Information on Squirrels. (n.d.). https://www.pestworld.org/news-hub/pest-articles/squirrels-101/

Staying Safe Around Bears - Bears (U.S. National Park Service). (n.d.). https://www.nps.gov/subjects/bears/safety.htm

Tim Knight - University of Washington. (n.d.). American Black Bear Facts for Kids - NatureMapping. http://naturemappingfoundation.org/natmap/facts/american_black_bear_k6.html

What to Do if You Encounter a Coyote | City of Edmonton. (n.d.). https://www.edmonton.ca/residential_neighbourhoods/pets_wildlife/what-to-do-if-you-encounter-a-coyote

White-Tailed Deer - WildlifeNYC. (n.d.). https://www.nyc.gov/site/wildlifenyc/animals/deer.page

Brown, T., & Morgan, A. B., Jr. (2023, April 4). Making cordage from natural materials. Mother Earth News – The Original Guide To Living Wisely; Mother Earth News. https://www.motherearthnews.com/diy/making-cordage-natural-materials-zmaz83jfzraw/

(2006, July 4). 3 ways to make a spear. WikiHow. https://www.wikihow.com/Make-a-Spear

How to make a fishing spear. (n.d.). Hedgehog Leatherworks. https://hedgehogleatherworks.com/blogs/blog/how-to-make-a-fishing-spear

Making survival traps. (2020, May 11). The Survival University. https://thesurvivaluniversity.com/survival-tips/wilderness-survival-tips/survival-traps/

O'Dea, M. (2023, September 27). 14 wilderness survival tools you should always have in your pack. The Dyrt Magazine. https://thedyrt.com/magazine/gear/wilderness-survival-tools/

Primitive Stone Tools. (n.d.). Alderleaf Wilderness College. https://www.wildernesscollege.com/primitive-stone-tools.html

Wilderness Arena. (2015, December 31). How to build primitive weapons and tools from natural bone, rocks, shells, antlers, or animal teeth - geek. Geek Slop. https://www.geekslop.com/life/survival/tools-supplies/2015/how-to-build-primitive-weapons-and-tools-from-natural-bone-rocks-shells-antlers-or-animal-teeth

Bites and stings – first aid. (n.d.). Gov.au. https://www.betterhealth.vic.gov.au/health/healthyliving/bites-and-stings-first-aid

Camping and hiking first aid kits. (n.d.). Elastoplast.co.uk. https://www.elastoplast.co.uk/did-you-know/health-and-protection/camping-and-hiking-first-aid-kit

Children's Health. (n.d.). Snake bites and children: What to do. Childrens.com. https://www.childrens.com/health-wellness/snake-bites-and-children-what-to-do

How to handle an emergency. (n.d.). Kidshealth.org. https://kidshealth.org/en/kids/emergency.html

Omohundro, N. (2021, May 20). DIY outdoor first aid kit & checklist. Little Family Adventure. https://littlefamilyadventure.com/diy-outdoor-first-aid-kit-checklist/

Aga, & Aga. (2018). How To Mark Trails Like A Pro. American Gun Association. https://blog.gunassociation.org/mark-trails-like-pro/

Dempsey, C. (2021). How to Read a Map. GIS Lounge. https://www.gislounge.com/making-maps-easier-to-read/

Direction. (n.d.). https://education.nationalgeographic.org/resource/direction/

McKay, B. K. (2021). How to Find Direction Using the Sun and Stars. The Art of Manliness. https://www.artofmanliness.com/skills/outdoor-survival/find-direction-without-compass/

Notes on Cardinal Directions. (2022, July 20). Unacademy. https://unacademy.com/content/cat/study-material/data-interpretation-and-logical-reasoning/cardinal-directions/

10 Household Items That Can Double as Survival Gear. (n.d.). Mossy Oak. https://www.mossyoak.com/our-obsession/blogs/10-household-items-that-can-double-as-survival-gear

10 secrets of successful wildlife watching — WildSweden - wildlife adventures in Sweden. (n.d.). WildSweden - Wildlife Adventures in Sweden. https://www.wildsweden.com/about/10-secrets-of-successful-wildlife-watching

John. (2023, May 7). Get Prepared: How to Survive When Lost in The Wilderness? Tactical Backpacks and Military Gears! https://www.tacticalogy.com/lost-in-wilderness-survival-guide/

Observing Wildlife | Wildlife Journal Junior. (n.d.). https://nhpbs.org/wild/observing.asp

ReadyWise. (n.d.). Staying Calm in Emergencies. ReadyWise. https://readywise.com/blogs/readywise-blog/staying-calm-in-emergencies

Signaling | Be Ready Utah. (n.d.). https://beready.utah.gov/family-preparedness/12-areas-of-preparedness/communication/signaling/

Survival psychology | Meaning, Definition, Origin. (n.d.). Survival Kompass. https://survival-kompass.de/dictionary/survival-psychology/

Top 10 Outdoor Survival Skills and Hacks. (n.d.). https://www.reserveamerica.com/articles/hiking/top-10-outdoor-survival-skills-and-hacks

Made in the USA
Las Vegas, NV
19 October 2024

97071465R00056